MERRY CHRISTMAS 1997

TO: KATIE,

WE LOVE YOU VERY MUCH & WE HOPE YOU
SPEND MANY HAPPY HOURS WITH THIS BOOK
& MANY HAPPY YEARS ENJOYING THE ENDLESS
BEAUTY OF NATURE.

Love,

Grandpa Fred &
Grandma Edna

Garden Butterflies
of North America

GARDEN BUTTERFLIES OF NORTH AMERICA

A Gallery of Garden Butterflies & How to Attract Them

by

Rick Mikula

Claudia Mikula, Editor

WILLOW CREEK PRESS

Minocqua, Wisconsin

KEY TO RANGE MAPS

Breeding range, usually spring and summer

Each species has a home range in which they may be found. Some species experience a summer time migration to northern reaches, only to perish there. They may not really be considered to be indigenous to the north; they can still be found as they stray into the region. Many guide books do not reflect the current resident populations. With more and more people watching and collecting data about butterflies, species are being found in areas where they were not previously. We have tried to capture and highlight the areas where particular species can most often be found.

PHOTOGRAPHY CREDITS

All photographs by the author except: William B. Folsom, pages 2, 31 (bottom), 74 (bottom), and 124 (bottom); John Shaw, pages 6, 23, 25 (top left), 42, 46 (top), 74 (top), 84 (top), 92 (top), 104 (top), 108 (bottom), 112 (bottom), 126 (both), 130 (bottom), and 132 (top); David Liebman, pages 8 (both), 11, 24, 25 (bottom right), 28 (top), 30 (bottom), 31 (top), 40 (top), 45 (bottom left), 62 (both), 64 (bottom), 66 (top), 112 (top), 114 (top), 116 (top), and 130 (top); Robert McCaw, pages 14 (top), 37 (bottom), 64 (top), and 78 (bottom), 90 (both), 92 (bottom), 94 (top), 96 (bottom), 100 (bottom), 102 (top), and 104 (bottom); Unicorn Stock Photos: Les Van, page 14 (bottom), Charles E. Schmidt, page 72 (top), and Dede Gilman, pages 114 (bottom) and 132 (bottom); Larry West, pages 15, 27, 78 (top), 84 (bottom), 86 (top), 94 (bottom), and 116 (bottom); Jeff Richter, pages 17, 18-19 spread, 34 (top), 36 (top and bottom), 37 (top), 48-49 spread, and 57; Bill Beatty, pages 20 and 134; Photo/Nats: Jeff March, page 28 (bottom); Kim Todd, page 33; Priscilla Connell, pages 40 (bottom), 47, 66 (bottom), and 98 (top); Tim Daniel, page 45 (top right); Gay Bumgarner, page 46 (bottom), and Muriel V. Williams, page 108 (top); Jeff March Nature Photography, pages 29 (bottom) and 136 (top); Bill Lea, pages 32 (top), 41, and 43; Jerry Zeidler, page 118 (both); Thomas C. Boyden, pages 22, 76 (both), and 82 (bottom), 86 (bottom), 88, 96 (top), 100 (top), 102 (bottom), 138 (both), and 140 (both); Dave Tylka, pages 53 and 60; Robert Campbell, pages 25 (top right), 70 (top), 82 (top), 98 (bottom), 106 (bottom), 122, 124 (top), and 136 (bottom); International Stock / J. Contreras Chacel, page 51; CEI Imaging / Picture Library Association, page 68; J. M. Fengler, page 72 (bottom); Paul Opler, pages 80 (both) and 110 (both); Jeffrey M. Young, page 106 (top); Jim P. Brock, page 120; Whit Bronaugh, page 128 (both); and Leroy Simon, page 70 (bottom).

Published by WILLOW CREEK PRESS,
P.O. Box 147, Minocqua, WI 54548

For information on other Willow Creek titles,
write or call 1-800-850-WILD.

Design by Patricia Bickner Linder.

Library of Congress Cataloging-in-Publication Data

Mikula, Rick.
    Garden butterflies of North America : a gallery of garden butterflies & how to attract them / by Rick Mikula ; Claudia Mikula, editor.
    p.   cm.
    ISBN 1-57223-086-x (alk. paper)
    1. Butterflies--North America. 2. Butterfly gardening--North America. I. Mikula, Claudia. II. Title.
QL548.M54   1997
595.78'9'097--dc21   97-8246
                                                                              CIP

Printed in Canada

CONTENTS

DEDICATION

hen my study of *lepidoptera* was in the egg stage, Claudia carefully nutured it. With patience, she allowed it to develop into a ravenous information-devouring entity. She was kind enough to feed it her knowledge of botany, horticulture and photography.

The growing entity needed rest and time to digest years of knowledge. The resting chrysalis churned, longing to explode into the outside world. It needed to spread its wings and take flight. Knowing the time was not right, she used tenderness and encouragement to pacify it. When emergence was finally inevitable, she stood back as the creature unfurled its wings and took to the sky. She stood in the background humble, knowing, and approving. Purposely not taking any light or the wind from its wings, she allowed it to go free.

I do not think Claudia will ever realize that my life with butterflies would not have been possible without her. Without her guidance over the years this book would not have been written. It was she who let the idea develop, mature, and fly. So it is with this dedication that I give thanks to the one person most responsible for this book being published. It was she who allowed me to fly.

With all my love.

A TRIBUTE
THE REGAL FRITILLARY

 n 1917 Clarence M. Weed chose to begin his book *Butterflies Worth Knowing* with a lithograph of the Regal Fritillary. Of it he wrote, "showing the marvelous sheen of its iridescence, it furnishes one of the most beautiful exhibitions of color in the world of nature."

Anyone who has been fortunate to see the Regal will never argue the point. When the sunlight intersects with the wing surface, it creates a royal purple crown of light. It is quite the "regal" fritilllary indeed. But that reward is only for a limited few. Every year more of its specialized habitat is lost, and sightings become rarer. In an 1898 edition of *The Butterfly Book*, W.J. Holland wrote, "This exceedingly beautiful insect ranges from Maine to Nebraska . . . at times it seems apparently common." Now nothing can be further from the truth. In less than a hundred years it has become extinct in New England.

There are many theories as to why the population is plummeting. The spraying of DDT in the 1950s and 1960s for gypsy moths may have been an important factor in New England. In the other states where the Regal once lived, the loss of wetland may be the culprit. That is why the Regal Fritillary should be the poster child for all North American butterflies. It is rapidly losing the battle against human encroachment. There are still strongholds in the Midwest, but that is only as long as the areas stay large, open grasslands. Butterflies are not as adaptable as humans, who could easily change the amber waves of a prairie into the hard black macadam of a mall parking lot. If we are not careful, they will soon go the way of the Palos Verde Blue. At the end, it lived in a habitat the size of a baseball field. So the city of Rancho Palos Verdes did just that, turned the area into a baseball field. In return we lost those marvelous winged specks of lapis. They are now extinct.

Another case in point is the Schaus' Swallowtail, the Key's Swallowtail. Even at its peak, it was found in Florida. But it enjoyed a particular section of real estate, that began to shrink. Today it can only be found in captivity, where the remaining population is kept isolated. Efforts are being made to keep the species alive, before it joins the ranks of those that are no more.

Similar attempts are underway in New England to restore the Regal to its throne. The last known New England poplulation became extinct in 1990. Some universities have banded together for a reintroduction program. Likely sites include Nantucket and Martha's Vineyard. The basic restocking, however, had to be butterflies imported from Pennsylvania. After many attempts, they successfully began to breed in captivity, and now the plan continues.

I am indeed privileged to be able to visit the last wild population of Regal Frits east of the Mississippi. The habitat is as beautiful as the butterflies that so desperately need it. Perhaps in a hundred years someone will quote me as to how decimated the Regal population once was. Hopefully this will be in contrast to the large colonies that will exist in the future.

Newly emerged
Regal Fritillary, right.

INTRODUCTION

ime has always been measured by various means, forever indexing our lives into smaller and smaller units. Calendars, clocks, and nanoseconds constantly remind us of where we should have been. In our hectic days, many important things around us unfortunately go unnoticed. In the lush mountains of northeastern Pennsylvania where I live, the measure of time is a thing of natural beauty.

As winter rolls back its blanket of snow, the slumbering vegetation beneath begins its springtime stretch. Soon, the most eager of all the wildflowers begin to bloom. By mid-April, the trout lily and bloodroot are there to welcome the violas. Wood anemone, columbine, and woodland phlox eventually round out the vernal landscape, setting the stage for another season.

Eventually, the warmer sun of May persuades the trees to unfold their bouquets. Lindera and lilacs always yield rich rewards, as does the Dutchman's pipe. They play host to the mountain's most beautiful visitors, the butterflies, which arrive just as Mother Nature begins to bloom.

If you want to know where the butterflies are, you must first know where their nourishment is. It is not just the blossoming garden flowers of July. The sources of butterfly nourishment vary with the season.

Many people think that "butterfly season" is only from June to September. Ironically, some species of butterflies ride out the northern winters by hibernating as adults. The first spring day that temperatures reach fifty-five degrees, they will take to the wing. Below that mark they'll be found clinging to loose bark on trees, in wood piles, and even in the eaves of houses.

Occasionally, a sudden, premature warm spell will seduce them from their haunts long before the springtime flowers are in bloom. On such a day, find a maple or oak tree that has a weeping wound or split root. The dripping sap is eagerly devoured by such butterflies as Angle Wings, Tortoise Shells, and Mourning Cloaks, as these early-season aviators perform their test flights.

The flowering spring blossoms help protect the butterflies with color camouflage. The earliest of the field flowers are yellow and white. This is a great benefit to the Sulphurs and Whites, which seem to become invisible as they alight on the flowers for brunch. Soon *Onacheewa*, the warm winds of spring, are replaced by the heat of summer, and things begin to accelerate.

And when things start to speed up, it's time to observe butterfly behavior closely. Stand at the edge of any field and watch the butterfly ballet. The first movement of the

recital is the "spiral dance," used by female white butterflies to discourage unwanted suitors. The male approaches the female and they begin to circle each other. As they continue to spiral, they rise nearly out of sight. Suddenly one of them will close its wings and drop straight to the ground. When the blindness of potential love finally clears from the suitor's eye, it realizes it was abandoned. It then drifts slowly to the ground with nothing more than a broken heart.

There are other stories and dancers in the field. As you watch, suddenly a butterfly flushes from the coltsfoot, then another darts from the chickweed. Then, before you know it, the entire field is alive with what appears to be flying flowers. It is the impression they gave to the Native Americans, who called them just that — flying flowers. In the Midwest, Native Americans referred to butterflies as "fluttering wings."

As the cycle continues, take a leisurely walk down a forgotten logging road or along a river bank and watch chips of blue spark up ahead of you. They are the Spring Azure and the Tailed Blue. Appearing to be the most fragile of all the butterflies, you'll find these rugged little flashes of lapis about wherever there is any sunlight.

The transition from spring to summer is customarily marked by the blooming of the lilacs, which anyone fortunate enough to have in their garden knows the wonderful gift they bestow. Tiger Swallowtails can not resist lilacs. Their yellow-and-black-striped wings harmonize so perfectly with the delicate lavender of the lilac spray.

Soon afterward, every garden and field is stirring with the colored wings of various butterflies soaring above them. They hurry about as if they are making ready for the return of the champion of all butterflies — the entrance of the Monarch.

At top, Monarchs migrating in southern Ontario; left, newly emerged Monarch.

GARDEN BUTTERFLIES OF NORTH AMERICA

After a winter siesta in Mexico, *Danaus plexippus*, the Monarch butterfly, once again inhabits the landscape. Although they take center stage, their brilliant colors dissolve into the milkweeds and clovers. Their arrival marks the height of summer, and all the players assume their roles. If you should happen to catch a Fritillary, which looks similar to a Monarch, count the number of silver spots on the underside of its wings. That is how much money you will come into, according to Appalachian Mountain folklore. It is those same silver dots that will help you determine if the orange splash hovering above the emerald field is a Frit or a Monarch.

In the northern climes, the butterfly activity begins winding down at the end of July. One morning it is just a little bit cooler and the sun seems to wake up a little bit later. The Joe-Pye weed enters and exits. The heliotrope quarters the sedum in preparation for the final movement in this symphony of colors. Although every thistle is bejeweled with a kaleidoscope of visitors, the eternal cycle commands respect. The clovers and bindweeds soon bow their heads and bid adieu to the ragweeds and goldenrod, who pick up the chorus for the finale. As nectar is transferred from one flower to the next, the butterflies follow these cues and do what they were meant to. Knowing this cycle of events will keep you in touch with the butterflies. Nectaring and pollinating, the butterflies scurry about, anticipating the fall of the winter curtain over the entire production.

In Pennsylvania, September is the best month of the year for enjoying butterflies. The last broods of certain species are preparing for wintry slumber. The migrating Monarchs hang like clusters of grapes on golden blooms as they store energy for the pilgrimage to Mexico. As the golden and scarlet leaves of autumn begin to fall, chrysalides and cocoons quickly assume their positions. Nooks and crannies soon become filled with pupae. Wood piles and tree hollows seem a mighty tempting alternative to winter's bitter winds. It is time to fort up for the long, frosty months ahead.

Great Spangled Fritillary on Orange Milkweed. According to Appalachian Mountain folklore, if you catch a fritillary, count the silver spots and that is how much money you will come into.

Author has butterflies timed
to hatch on his Christmas tree
each year.

The long winter months do not mean that the butterflies are gone. They are everywhere in the woods and garden. The trick is knowing where to look and what to look for. With a little practice, you will become quite adept at locating chrysalides and cocoons in their winter digs. And it makes a wonderful wintertime treasure hunt that the whole family can enjoy together. In the process, you'll also discover the beauty the woods have to offer at an otherwise dismal time of year.

The Douglas fir, blue spruce, and Scotch pine remind us that our colorful friends are still at our fingertips. It is not often that a Christmas goes by that someone somewhere in the country calls to tell of a miracle that has just happened. No matter how many times it happens it is still marvelous to hear. A family will buy a Christmas tree and stand it in a place of honor. Then, a few days later, a butterfly is flying around their house.

This is not as bizarre as it sounds. When butterflies are ready to pupate, they search for a comfortable location. Evergreens (Christmas trees, in many cases) make a wise choice because they offer protection against winds and early thaws. Thinking all is right with the world, the butterfly begins its hibernation. Once the tree is felled and placed in a warm house, the butterfly, thinking it is spring, does what comes naturally. It emerges and delights everyone.

At the most dismal part of winter, when most folks are developing cabin fever, spring begins. It's at this time that designing a butterfly garden is quite fulfilling. By choosing which species we intend to invite to our oasis, we develop our gardening plan. The garden is our palette and the flowers are our paint. Allowing the colors to swirl in your mind offers a stimulating alternative to late winter's grays and browns. It is also time to start seeds and cuttings.

I have learned to use the flora and fauna as my calendar to tell me where the butterflies will be. *"Half past the coneflowers and a quarter to the buddleia"* means that the butterfly season is about to get under way. Dogbane going to seedhead means the field clover will be getting ripe and active with flying jewels — the height of the season. Finally, the asters and weeds take to the air for a golden good-bye as the season begins to wind down to the final curtain call.

Every year *Onacheewa*, the warm winds of spring, return once more. Upon these warm winds the rainbow of butterflies can spread its wings and fly. As they take to the sky, the cycle is renewed.

Rick Mikula

BUTTERFLY GARDENS OF NORTH AMERICA

umans have always been fascinated by butterflies. They are depicted in Bronze Age frescoes and in prehistoric cave drawings. The Greeks paid tribute to the butterfly with the Goddess Psyche. Half woman/half butterfly, she represented the soul. Other cultures took the mythology a step further, believing that their souls would be borne to heaven on the wings of butterflies. Butterflies even decorate the tombs of Imperial Rome, signifying the soul's transition to the afterlife. The belief is kept alive to this day with Mexico's Festival of the Dead, in which butterflies signify the souls of dead children coming back to visit their relatives.

In Victorian England butterflies were a passion, as the many butterfly atriums and conservatories in existence then attested. Many great explorers were commissioned to venture to uncharted parts of the world to collect exotic butterfly species. In modern England, butterflies served a less-fanciful purpose, at least for Roger Banister, the first human to run a mile in less than four minutes. He trained for such a feat by chasing butterflies and catching them with his hands!

Butterflies are part of our lives more than we realize. Who among us cannot remember being fascinated by a "flutter-by" as we chased it through our gardens?

Even Native Americans were fascinated with these winged beauties. Sitting Bull, the most famous of all Native American chiefs, had a Monarch butterfly fixed to his ceremonial head dress.

America's love affair with butterflies grows stronger each year, even expanding outside the United States. Butterfly houses and live exhibits are emerging faster than chrysalides in August. Newspapers and magazines around the world are filled with lepidopteran tales, and butterflies have even emerged on the World Wide Web. Fortunately, it appears that a long-lasting relationship is being established between people and butterflies.

HOW DO YOU SAY BUTTERFLY?

Every language has a different word for butterfly. Some names sound beautiful and delicate; others are almost humorous. Here are a few that have been collected from around the world. How many do you recognize?

Anglo-Saxon	*butterfloege*	Japanese	*choo*
Arabic	*farasha*	Korean	*nahby*
Bundjalung	*banjalahm*	Latin	*papilio*
Cherokee	*kamama*	Malaysian	*rama-rama*
Czech	*motyl*	Norwegian	*sommerfugl*
Danish	*sommerfugl*	Nyungar	*bataplai*
Dutch	*vlinder*	Polish	*motyl*
Esperanto	*papilio*	Portuguese	*borboleta*
Finnish	*perhonen*	Rumanian	*fluture*
French	*papillon*	Russian	*babochka*
German	*schmetterling*	Serbo-Croat	*leptir*
Greek	*petalouda*	Spanish	*mariposa*
Hawaiian	*pulelehua*	Swahili	*kipepeo*
Hebrew	*parpar*	Swedish	*fjaril*
Hungarian	*lepke*	Tagala	*paru-paru*
Indonesian	*kupu-kupu*	Turkish	*kelebek*
Italian	*farfalla*	Yiddish	*chmetterling*

Eastern Tiger Swallowtail on zinnia, left; American Painted Lady on Black-eyed Susan, right.

THE LIFE CYCLE OF A BUTTERFLY

Unfortunately most people do not understand what comes first: the butterfly or the egg. Some folks do not have a clue that an egg stage is even involved in the butterfly's life cycle. In our rushed society, not many of us have the time to devote to butterfly life cycles. It is, however, a simple system that is easy to follow.

The day after a female emerges from her chrysalis, she is ready to mate. In fact, it is usually hard to find a female over two or three days old that has not mated. Zebra Longwing males do not even wait until the female is free of the chrysalis. The males, in all their eagerness, will actually assist in removing the female, mate, and then be gone. It's not the lovely "mate for life" scheme demonstrated by Canadian geese and other wild creatures.

After mating, the female searches for the proper host plant and begins to deposit her eggs. Young, tender hosts are chosen, because the female knows that her brood will have fresh, succulent leaves to devour.

Usually, in a few days the caterpillar will emerge from the egg. Depending on the species, the caterpillar stage may last from a week to several months. The caterpillar is an eating machine, gobbling its way to the pupal stage. Most moths construct a cocoon, but most butterflies form a naked chrysalis. Timing is species-specific. Some butterflies emerge from a chrysalis in a week, while others may take years. But when the proper moment is reached, the butterfly springs free of its chamber, and the cycle continues.

So what we have is the basic cycle of egg, caterpillar, chrysalis, and, finally, adult butterfly. Eggs may be referred to as ova, the caterpillars can be called larvae, and pupa is another word for chrysalis. The adult stage is sometimes called the imago. It does not matter if you use the words egg, caterpillar, chrysalis and adult, or ovum, larva, pupa, and imago; only one thing is important. To spend time enjoying these creatures.

Milbert's Tortoise Shell eggs, top left, mature larva of the Pipevine Swallowtail, top right, and pupa of Variegated Fritillary, below; Cloudless Sulphur caterpillar feeding, left.

GARDEN BUTTERFLIES OF NORTH AMERICA

WHY DO BUTTERFLIES BASK?

By nature, the butterfly is cold-blooded. Most Lepidoptera cannot fly if it is below fifty degrees. In order to fly they must warm their internal muscles to eighty degrees. There are several ways this can be accomplished.

Basking is a much-needed activity for butterflies. The adult finds a nice sunny spot and lets the sun do the work. A light-colored surface is preferred by adults, because sunlight is reflected from the surface and the insect is warmed from below as well as from above. Basking becomes a ritual with some species. Some hold their wings at only certain angles. Others tilt or contort their bodies into what they consider the most advantageous pose. Certain species can even be identified at a distance by the position they assume when basking.

Light-colored stones, sand, or a sidewalk may provide an adequate spot. One of my favorites is called a waterless pond. To construct one is fairly easy. First, choose some white or light-colored stones. The diameter of the stones determines the depth of the pond. And it is best if the stones are fairly uniform in size. Next, dig an indentation into the ground. I prefer to make it in the outline of a butterfly. Line the hole with plastic and then place the stones into it. There's no need to fill it with water. The morning dew will collect onto the rocks and slowly drip to the plastic at the bottom, where it will be collected for the day.

Purplish Copper basking in sunshine.

As butterflies go to the site to bask, they will discover the water. With tongues or a "proboscis" that are sometimes longer than they are, the butterflies can easily retrieve the protected moisture. At day's end the water has evaporated and does not offer a place for bacteria and mold to develop. The next day the water is fresh once again.

One large rock placed in your birdbath is just as effective. It offers water and basking at the same time. A pan or tray of moist sand will work quite satisfactorily, too, but placing a salt block in the center makes it even more inviting. Experiment. You may even surprise yourself with an ingenious creation.

THE BASIC INGREDIENTS

The more our gardens resemble a wildflower meadow the more attractive they will be to butterflies. Unfortunately, local zoning boards may not find this acceptable, and the neighbors may complain about the uncut grass. But the butterflies will love it. After all, which is more important?

Most people desire order in their lives and they translate that into their garden scheme. But a meadow theme can still be used and will appear maintained. Your lawn is already a miniature meadow containing many fine host plants such as dandelion, plantain, and clovers. In fact, every time you mow your lawn you may be killing butterflies in the form of eggs or caterpillars. The state of New Hampshire realized that by simply raising the blade height of the mowers used along its highways, it saved the lives of endangered Blue butterflies.

In our gardening plan we must address each stage of the butterfly's life cycle. We must supply host plants for the female to lay her eggs on and in sufficient amounts to carry the larva through its development period. Shrubs, grasses, and other uprights offer the caterpillars places to form their chrysalis. The newly emerged adult will see no reason to leave this habitat, because of the nectar plants available. Our garden should also provide water and shelter. A site for basking is not essential, but it's pleasant to look at, and basking is an important part of the adult's life. Supplying these needs to butterflies is much easier than you might imagine.

The style of your butterfly garden is totally under your control. You may go with annuals and redecorate every season. You may desire to plant only perennials. (The best butterfly garden is a combination of both.)

Remember, the garden is your canvas and the flowers are your palette. It is up to you to create a masterpiece. And any friendly habitat is much needed by butterflies. They cannot tell you, but they will show their appreciation — in vivid colors.

COVER

Where do butterflies go when it rains? I wish I had a Fritillary for ever time I was asked that question. During rainy periods butterflies seek any available shelter. It may be under leaves or among vegetation. The eaves of houses, or a stone fence will do in times of need. But rain is not the only

Supply host plants for butterflies to lay eggs on as well as nectar plants for feeding.

A garden sanctuary provides a place
for butterflies to seek protection
when it rains.

reason that butterflies seek sanctuary. Many species hibernate in winter, which also requires shelter and cover. There are several ways in which we can provide butterflies with protection in our gardens.

Except for certain areas, the prevailing wind in the United States is from the northwest. Orienting the garden so that the tallest plants are at the northern perimeter and the shortest

are at the southern edge provides cover. If you have existing shrubs that will be incorporated in your garden, use the shrubs as a northern windbreak for the garden. Your house or another existing structure works as a windbreak also. Fences, mounds of earth, and fountains are excellent starting points for planting tall windbreak plants. Whatever is used, make sure that it will take the brunt of the prevailing wind in your area and shelter the garden.

If your landscape slopes, you have an advantage. Not only will it offer protection from breezes, but it tilts the carpet of flowers, making their colors visible to butterflies at a greater distance. Raised beds can be placed in strategic locations and make an attractive presentation while still serving their original purpose of protection. They are easy to maintain and can be hand-groomed for unwanted insects.

If your land is flat, proper wind protection is still easily available. That's where shrubs, trees, and fences come in handy. A simple, inexpensive alternative is a pile of stones or logs (stacked firewood), which creates cover and a natural habitat. Please use caution before throwing a log into the fire. Check it for any chrysalis and adults. Many Anglewing and Tortoise Shell butterflies hide beneath the loose bark of logs.

A lovely item on the market is the "Butterfly House," which should actually be called a "hibernating box." Butterfly houses originated in Scotland where many butterflies overwinter in the adult stage. The box has long, narrow slots, suggesting a tree hollow or crevice. They will be most productive if placed in a wooded or shady section of your landscape. Butterflies that use hibernating boxes prefer nettles, hops, willows, and elms. So if the box is placed near any of these, its effectiveness will increase. Usually the boxes have natural wood sides. It helps if you paint tiny purple and yellow flowers on the outside, because butterflies are

A raised-bed butterfly garden can be both useful and attractive as demonstrated at Dollywood in Pigeon Forge, Tennessee, top; check for chrysalides before throwing a log on the fire, bottom.

triggered by visual cues and the patterns will get their attention. It also looks nice and makes a great conversation piece when you're lounging on the deck.

Butterfly hibernating boxes can be made very easily at home. They really do not have to follow specific measurements as with birdhouses. Most important is the choice of wood used for construction. Avoid cedar because of its repelling properties. Your best bet is good old cheap pine. It may not wear like other woods, but if you have to replace it every five or ten years, big deal! It will give you the opportunity to redesign it.

Most people get butterfly boxes in the early spring when gardening fever begins. They put the box in the garden and are disappointed because it did not immediately attract butterflies. If used at all, the boxes won't be inhabited until late fall and winter.

FOOD

The best part of planting a butterfly garden is that you decide what goes into it. There are many plants that are attractive to butterflies, and most are readily available. However, one of your first considerations in choosing plants should be color.

Butterflies see color in the ultraviolet spectrum through amazingly complex eyes, which also see in many different directions at once to detect predators. When humans look at a Black-eyed Susan, we see yellow and brown. To the wondrous eye of a butterfly, the same flower shines brilliant blues and silvers for quite a distance. To the many-faceted eyes of these insects, every nuance of color becomes an intricate mosaic. The colors of the flowers aid in attracting butterflies that in turn help to pollinate the plant.

Butterflies have certain color preferences. Purple, pink, yellow, white, blue, and red seem to be the order in which colors are appreciated by the butterflies of North America.

When planting, strive to offer a constant source of blooming nectar plants throughout the flight season. Do not plant flowers that will only bloom in the early spring and wonder where the butterflies are in August. Plants such as sedum bloom later and are greatly appreciated by lingering individuals. As one plant dies, another should be there for the butterflies.

Cabbage White flicks at bumble bee on lilac, top; American Painted Lady on May Night Hybrid Sage.

Consult the regional plant list to find flowers that grow best in your area; for example, purple coneflowers grow well in the Northeast, top.

Water is very important to butterflies and can be provided in a number of attractive ways, bottom.

Many well-intentioned, would-be butterfly gardeners opt for shortcuts, planting flowers and seeds among weeds. They never have a chance, because the weeds quickly displace the flowers. There really are no shortcuts to a successful butterfly garden. But it's not that difficult either, especially if you consult the regional plant lists on page 35.

Whichever plants you decide on, make sure they are a combination of host as well as nectar plants. Nectar plants will attract butterflies; host plants will keep them there. Once the female finds food, she will begin to deposit her eggs. Flowering plants should be placed in clusters or groups. Insect-deterring plants should be placed among the other plants as organic pest controls. In conjunction with hand grooming, it provides a chemical-free environment.

WATER

We were always told that if a butterfly got a drop of water on it, it would die. Bilge water! Actually, water is extremely important to butterflies. Humidity is needed to assist them in emerging from the egg. When thirsty, caterpillars nibble on the stem of moist plants. Adults need water almost as much as nectar. And they are much more water-repellent than one would think. If an adult is submersed at the bottom of a water bucket, upon release it will float to the top and fly away. Adults actively seek out water. In fact, it is not unusual to see butterflies flying in light rain, almost seeming to enjoy the shower.

A water source can take various forms in a butterfly garden. Bird baths, ponds, or even an overturned trash-can lid buried in the ground will supply ample amounts of water. Fountains and "bubbling rocks" are the most attractive, but a pond or puddle serves best. If you decide on a pond or puddle, surround it with light-colored stones or sand. Not only does it dress up the water source a bit, it offers a basking (warming) site for butterflies. During very hot weather, spraying your garden plants with a hose is a delight for butterflies.

Moisture can also be provided with a pan of wet sand, the best of which is salt-saturated beach sand, which is important to males for the production of sperm. By using beach sand you will also be establishing a place for the "guys" to hang out, swap stories, and catch up on the latest nectaring site before they set out to cruise for females. The salty sand is also good for keeping pesky snails and slugs from invading host plants and killing caterpillars.

Midwesterners may find that going to the seashore for sand is a little expensive. But the feed store may only be a hop, skip, and a jump away. Buy a salt or mineral block that is used for livestock, place it next to your garden's watering site and it will take care of itself. The morning dew will dissolve a little bit every day. Placing the block on a wooden surface will cause the salt to leech into the wood and last longer. However you decide to provide water to your butterflies is up to you. The important thing is that water is available for them.

Eastern Tiger Swallowtail puddling in Guadalupe Mountains National Park in Texas.

Flowers should be planted in clusters or clumps for best results, as butterflies find protection in windbreaking shrubbery.

THE PLAN

Now that you know the basic ingredients for a successful garden, the next step is to draw a map of your property, showing the location of the house, garage, driveway, lawn, and all existing cover, such as trees, shrubs, hedges, ground cover, rock walls, and terrain. Inventory how much cover, food, and water you already have on your property. Now it's time to determine what you must plant, grow, build, add, and install to fulfill the needs of the butterflies you want to entice.

Make a list of the items you might need to convert your backyard into a butterfly paradise:

1. Windbreaking shrubbery or other tall plants.
2. Ground cover in which butterflies can hide, find protection from weather, and hibernate.
3. Flowers — annuals and/or perennials — of the color and type that attract the butterflies in your area.
4. Wild corners of the yard where the natural vegetation is allowed to grow into mini-wilderness.
5. Sloped or terraced areas that will expose flowers to butterflies at longer ranges.
6. Wood piles that offer butterflies cover and a place to hibernate.

GARDEN BUTTERFLIES OF NORTH AMERICA

Food and Cover Plants for Butterflies

Northeast

Bee Balm
Common milkweed
Loosestrife
Mexican sunflower
New England aster
New Jersey tea
Queen Anne's lace
Purple coneflower
Sedum
Thistle
Verbenas
Zinnia

Mid-Atlantic

Ageratum
Cleome
Coneflowers
Flame flower
Goldenrods
Hollyhock
Iron weed
Joe-pye weed
Lantana
Orange milkweed
Pipevine
Sweet fennel

West Coast

Anise
Bloodflower milkweed
Buckwheat
Deerweed
Hibiscus
Heliotrope
Lantana
Mimiosa
Monkey flower
Nasturtium
Passion flower
Rosemary

Pacific Northwest

Anise hyssop
Coreopsis
Dianthus
Lobelia
Pearly everlasting
Red valerian
Sedum
Showy milkweed
Sulphur flower
Thyme
Yarrow
Zinnia

Midwest

Boneset
Button bush
Catnip
Dogbane
Lataris
Lead plant
Marigold
Pagoda plant
Phlox
Purple milkweed
Sedum
Western wallflower

Southwest

Desert poppy
Lantana
Mimosa
Ox-eye daisy
Pepper grass
Pinchusion
Purple milkweed
Rabbit bush
Red valerian
Verbenas
Wild hyssop
Western aster

Upper Midwest

Cosmos
Marigold
Mexican hat
Mock orange
Lataris
Leadwort
Phlox
Porter's aster
Rocky Mountain wild lilac
Shasta daisy
Wallflower
Whorled milkweed

Southeast

Blazing star
Blue potterweed
Cassia
Green shrimp plant
Lantana
Mexican flame vine
Passiflora
Pentas Lanceolata
Pickerel weed
Red bay
Scarlet milkweed
Wild lime

Alaska

Ageratum
Alyssum
Bunchberry
Carrot family
Fireweed
Violets
Goatsbeard
Pipsissewa
Potentilla
Sedum
Tree Mallow
Zinnia

There is no question that buddleia, often referred to as "Butterfly Bush," is the absolute best butterfly-attracting plant in the world, and it can be found worldwide. From Australia to Atlanta, many people are seeing just how effective this plant can be. On a photographic expedition to Mt. Wai'ale'ale in Kauai, Hawaii, we were treated to a familiar sight. There, at an elevation of 4,000 feet stood a stand of buddleia covered with butterflies. The Gulf Fritillaries were busy courting and feeding, as the Skippers and Lantana butterflies came and went.

At my lectures and seminars, I always suggest planting buddleia. And it never fails that shortly afterward I receive a letter from a neophyte butterfly gardener who says while still digging the hole to plant their new buddleia, several butterflies landed on it. Buddleia is available in several colors, the best of which seems to be the "Black Knight." If you are trying to achieve a color pattern with your garden palette, choose the shade that fits into your color scheme. With buddleia you cannot go wrong.

Also, every ideal butterfly garden should have *Lantana camara.* It is an annual in the North, but will bloom all year in the South. To suggest Lantana to someone from Florida or Hawaii will naturally raise eyebrows. In Florida, Lantana gets, as Floridians say, "half as big as a house and twice as ugly." To me, Lantana cannot get too big. It is a valuable nectar plant ranking second only to buddleia. Obviously, Lantana can get too big. In Hawaii it got so big that in 1902, Larger and Smaller Lantana butterflies were introduced to curb its expansion. As with all other foreign introductions, it backfired. No one thought of the fact that the introduced species also consume garden crops. There is sure a lot more Lantana than there are Lantana butterflies in Hawaii, even after a century of co-existing. Lantana is number two on the top-ten list.

The third best nectar source is *Pentas lanceolata,* the Egyptian Star Flower. If you are fortunate enough to live where Pentas grow, you are the focus of my envy. Pentas is a beautiful flowering plant in any capacity that it is used. It is perfect for potting in colder climates. In a hanging basket or in floor pots, it is a valuable nectar source for all butterflies. I always find it amusing to browse through butterfly guidebooks and look at the pictures. One thing that stands out is how often a butterfly from some exotic part of the world is photographed on *Pentas lanceolata.* The untold story here is that the photos were taken at a butterfly zoo. Why travel the globe and spend thousands of dollars, when they can

Many plant species attract butterflies, such as these members of the Composite family (above) and creeping phlox (bottom)

all be had at a marvelous place such as the Day Butterfly Center at Calloway Gardens in Georgia? It's loaded with Pentas and butterflies.

Kept above fifty-five degrees, much like butterflies, Pentas will continue to bloom, even indoors. It is an excellent wintertime nectar provider. Pennsylvania winter temperatures can get down to fifteen degrees below zero. In the safety of our home, the little red faces of our Pentas just shine through our windows, converting sunshine into food.

The plant has adapted well to many locales. It is wonderful to stroll along California's Monterey Bay and discover plots of Pentas, or stumble into a patch along the Gulf Coast. Pentas and butterflies are a marvelous match. So if you live in an area that can support *Pentas lanceolata,* include it into your garden.

There are many other species of plants that may be better butterfly attractors in your area than the three mentioned here. Buttonbush in Texas will hold its own against any challenger.

It is always a good idea to contact a local expert, master gardener, or landscape designer for local tips. What works in Santa Fe may not work in Seattle. The three plants I've mentioned are the best nectar sources, in my estimation. Everyone has their favorites, but this triple-header is the work horse for nectaring adult butterflies.

Use a variety of colors in your garden scheme to attract more butterflies. Wild lupines, top; Silvery Blue butterfly on wild lupines, left.

PLANTING A BUTTERFLY GARDEN

This type of garden is best when positioned toward the sun. By planting various flowers, herbs, and shrubs of different heights, a wall of color is created. This will be more easily noticed by passing butterflies that will soon be beckoned to your oasis. The outside edges of the garden slope downward toward the front also. The lowest growing flowers should be planted closer to the water source. Stones and sand offer a much needed basking site.

The garden can be planted in a bowl effect surrounding your water source. The taller growing flowers would be placed at outer edge of the bowl. The lowest growing flowers would be planted closer to the center. By planting in this scheme, the structure of the garden offers protection from the wind. Butterflies can quickly dart from water to flower. Your lawn is probably filled with dandelion, plantain, and clover already. When used in conjunction with the nectar sources, your garden will be a butterfly paradise.

GARDEN BUTTERFLIES OF NORTH AMERICA

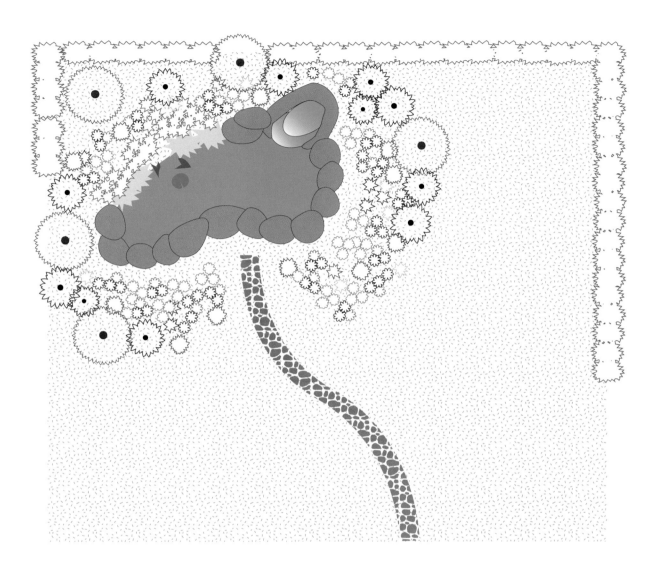

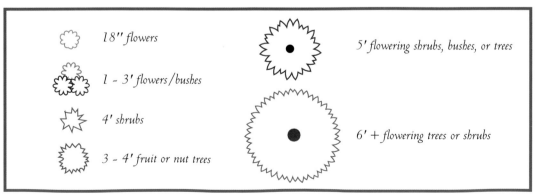

	18" flowers		5' flowering shrubs, bushes, or trees
	1 - 3' flowers/bushes		6' + flowering trees or shrubs
	4' shrubs		
	3 - 4' fruit or nut trees		

PLANTING BY REGION

Some flowers are good for butterflies and seem to grow everywhere. Other plants are only used by some butterflies in one area and not another. If you have the opportunity, find the butterflies in your area and note which plants they prefer. What humans find attractive may be totally unacceptable to a butterfly. They may not want to visit what we think they should like. By observing them in their natural habitat, you will be able to identify the plants that butterflies in your area prefer and duplicate those choices in your garden.

Unfortunately many top choices may be what we would consider weeds. In such cases we may want to opt for plants that are a little more tame. The types that are available at nurseries and plant shops make wonderful alternatives. The list of suggested plants on page 35 offers broad choices that should be readily available. They may not be the absolute best in your area, but to pinpoint every butterfly's taste in every area would be impossible. Latitude, humidity, available sunlight, and many other factors will determine nectar productivity and prime time, which may not coincide with that of a butterfly's. Plants that may be used by a larva in the southern section of a state or region may not be used by the same species in the northern part.

Trying to achieve a middle ground, we have chosen easy-to-find, low-maintenance plants that appeal to a wide assortment of our butterfly friends. The lists are a combination of perennials, annuals, and caterpillar host plants. Not only do we want to attract them to our garden, we would like them to deposit eggs there. And the luxury of having a few annuals affords us the opportunity to change some colors from year to year. Many host plants are herbs and annuals, which can be changed seasonally to invite various types of butterflies to the same locale.

If you do discover a flower that is irresistible to butterflies, share it with everyone you know. If others plant what you suggest, it will aid the butterflies in your area and may help to increase their numbers. By sharing, everyone will benefit from your knowledge. And you'll sleep well knowing that you have helped the most delicate of all creatures.

Hackberry butterfly caterpillar sunning and feasting, top; Zebra Longwing laying eggs on host plant, bottom; Firepink flowers, right.

Many insects pose problems for the butterfly gardener. Ants, aphids, and others may prey on caterpillars in your area and prevent them from reaching adult butterfly stage. Obviously, insecticides are out of the question. You could keep your caterpillars confined in netted pots of host plants and spray the garden. But why do that when there are a number of plants that naturally deter unwanted insects but are butterfly-friendly? Many of the insect-deterring plants are herbs. So plant plenty of them and both you and your butterflies will be the beneficiaries.

We all like to change our gardens from time to time, or perhaps add a few annuals to brighten up the scheme. The best use of these plants is to intermingle them with what's already planted. For example, marigolds or mints surrounding a patch of milkweed will keep it free of ants and aphids. Here's a list of some other important plant combinations that will give you both natural pest control and butterfly host plants.

Close-up view of Monarch egg on milkweed, right; planting milkweed and other butterfly-friendly plants will help eggs and caterpillars reach the adult butterfly stage.

PLANT	INSECT DETERRED	LARVAL HOST
Anise	Aphids	Yes
Aster	Most	Yes
Basil	Flies and Mosquitoes	No
Bee Balm	Most	No
Coriander	Aphids	No
Garlic	Japanese Beetle	No
Marigolds	Real Workhorse	Yes
Mints	Ants	Yes
Nasturtium	Aphids	Yes
Petunia	Most	No
Rosemary	Cabbage Moth	No
Rue	Japanese Beetle	Yes
Sage	Cabbage Moth	No
Tansy	Ants and Plant Lice	Yes

Bee Balm deters most insects harmful to butterflies.

Top 12
Perennials and Annuals
for Attracting Butterflies

Perennials

1.	Butterfly Bush	*Buddleia davidii*
2.	Butterfly Weed	*Asclepias tuberosa*
3.	Coreopsis	*Coreopsis auriculata*
4.	Hollyhock	*Althaea rosea*
5.	Lantana	*Lantana camara*
6.	Loosestrife	*Lythrum salicaria*
7.	New England Aster	*Aster novae-angliae*
8.	Phlox	*Phlox paniculata*
9.	Purple Coneflower	*Echinacea purpurea*
10.	Verbena	*Verbena bonariensis*
11.	Violet	*Viola*
12.	Yarrow	*Achillea millefolium*

Annuals

1.	Cosmos	*Cosmos bipinnatus*
2.	Heliotrope	*Heliotropium arborescens*
3.	Impatiens	*Impatiens balsamina/wallerana*
4.	Marigolds	*Tagetes tenifolia/patula*
5.	Mexican Sunflower	*Tithonia rotundifolia*
6.	Nasturtium	*Tropaeolum majus*
7.	Phlox	*Pholx spp.*
8.	Pin-Cushion	*Scabiosa caucasica*
9.	Shasta Daisy	*Chrysanthemum spp.*
10.	Sweet William	*Dianthus barbatus*
11.	Verbena	*Verbena hybrida/tenuisecta*
12.	Zinnia	*Zinnia elegans*

"BUDDY-FLY INSECTS"

Just as there are plants that deter insects that are harmful to butterflies, there are a number of insects that prey on their brethren that are harmful to butterflies. The trick is attracting them to your garden.

Sweet fennel, caraway, and dill are valuable caterpillar host plants that attract ladybugs and syrphids, the former of which is well known for its benefits in the garden. Two other plants — tansy and cosmos — attract both ladybugs and lacewing. Together they do an efficient job of keeping gardens clear of aphids, thrips, and spider mites, three insects that are harmful to butterflies.

Another efficient insect predator to invite into your garden is the dragonfly, which eats its own weight in mosquitoes every day. The invitation is simple. Just cut a piece of bamboo four to six feet long and push it in the ground about a foot. The upright bamboo will serve as a perch for dragonflies from which to ambush their prey.

Foot-long pieces of bamboo or pieces of old garden hose bundled and tied are a great trap for caterpillar-eating earwigs. Simply place the bundled pieces in your garden. At daybreak earwigs will crawl into the tubes. All you have to do is transfer the prisoners to a coffee can and place the can in the freezer for an hour or two.

Monarch resting near spider web, top; black and yellow Argiope spider preys on Tiger Swallowtail and Cabbage White.

HERBS AND THE BUTTERFLIES THEY ATTRACT

When herbs are in bloom, it is impossible to keep butterflies away. Unfortunately, many caterpillars find our herbs just as appetizing as we do. Yet butterflies and herbs can co-exist by simply planting more of everything. Not so easy? Try planting a few extra of the noted host herbs in separate containers and put your butterfly larvae on them by hand. Then cover them with netting to confine them. Problem solved.

Here are some of the most popular herbs and the butterflies they attract.

Spring Azure on violet, top; Hackberry butterfly on mint, bottom.

HOST HERB	ATTRACTED BUTTERFLY
Anise	Anise Swallowtails
Borage	Painted Ladys
Burdock	Painted Ladys
Caraway	Black Swallowtails
Clover	Sulphurs and Whites
Dill	Black Swallowtails
Dock	Coppers
Fennel	Anise and Black Swallowtails
Ginger (wild)	Pipevines
Hop vine	Tortoise Shells, Red Admirals
Hyssop (water)	White Peacocks
Lavendar	Anise and Black Swallowtails
Marjoram	Sootywings
Mallow	Painted Ladys, Hairstreaks, Skippers
Mints	Gray Hairstreak, Smaller Lantana
Mustard	Orange Tips, Marblewings
Nasturtium	Cabbage Whites, Spring Azures
Nettle	Question Marks, Commas, Red Admirals
Parsley	Black and Anise Swallowtails
Plantain	Variegated Fritillary, Checkerspots, Buckeyes
Rue	Black and Giant Swallowtails
Sassafras	Spicebush and Palamedes Swallowtails
Vervain	Checkerspots
Violet	Fritillaries
Yarrow	Black and Anise Swallowtails

Zebra Longwing eggs on passion vine;
Next page: field of wild lupines

GLIMPSES INTO
BUTTERFLY GARDENS OF NORTH AMERICA

The appreciation of butterflies grows by the day, which is why there are more and more butterfly "houses" around the world, several of which are in the U.S. If there isn't one near you now just wait, there is probably one scheduled for the future. Many zoological parks have added butterfly exhibits. A great way to find a butterfly house near you is by doing a search on the World Wide Web, where many butterfly houses have Web sites that allow you to take a virtual tour before you visit.

But without question, Pacific Grove, California, is considered "Butterfly Town USA." Nestled on Monterey Bay, it plays host to masses of migrating Monarch butterflies every autumn. While Eastern Monarchs journey to central Mexico for the winter, the western variety chooses the Monterey Bay area. Although there are many such sites scattered across central California, Pacific Grove is the showpiece.

Each fall as the Monarchs begin to return to this Victorian town, a magical time for children begins. To honor their orange-and-black guests, the children of Pacific Grove don the most enjoyable costumes. Dressed as chrysalides, caterpillars, and butterflies, they parade down the main street. It surely is not the biggest or grandest parade in the country, but it is certainly one of the more humorous. If the opportunity arises to see this parade, please do so. It is as touching as it is amusing, and worth the trip.

There are other reasons this butterfly berg deserves its name — the two butterfly-wintering groves within the city limits. But do not touch the butterflies, because doing so can result in a $500 fine. It may sound harsh, but the fine discourages would-be poachers. The city appreciates the winged visitors and honors them and the children with lovely statues throughout area.

Another not-so-famous site is Natural Bridges State Park near Santa Cruz, California. More formal than Pacific Grove, on the right day in Natural

Annual parade down Main Street of
"Butterfly Town USA,"
Pacific Grove, California, above.
Monarchs take flight, right.

GARDEN BUTTERFLIES OF NORTH AMERICA

Bridges Park it is like walking through a holy place. To see the eucalyptus trees laden with thousands and thousands of Monarch butterflies is truly awe-inspiring. They seem to disappear as they slowly open and close their wings. With wings closed, they blend perfectly with the summer-burnished leaves. But get a little too close and you will be warned with a flash of orange.

California's butterfly wintering sites range from Santa Barbara to Santa Cruz and points between. Many have not been discovered, while others have been destroyed. So as you walk softly through the central California landscape, do not be surprised if you discover a private site.

THE DAY BUTTERFLY CENTER

Seventy miles south of Atlanta, Georgia, stands the Cathedral of the Holy, in Calloway Gardens at Pine Mountain, Georgia. Under the direction of Frank Elia, the Day Butterfly Center is heaven on earth. Of all the butterfly exhibits I have had the good fortune to visit, this is my favorite.

The Day Butterfly Center is smaller than some but as intricate as any. A gentle pathway beckons one to glide through the butterfly house. Lush plants serve as resting spots for the most beautiful butterflies from around the world. Being surrounded by soothing music and colors, it is easy to forget the automated sprinkler system that may treat your camera to a bath. But it is worth the risk. Though some people feel that keeping butterflies in captivity is inappropriate, nothing could be further from the truth.

Butterflies live twice as long in captivity as they do in the wild. In the Day Butterfly Center's atrium, the butterflies are well fed and have plenty of

Statue honoring all the children that have taken part in the annual butterfly parade in Pacific Grove, California, top; Tree Nymph at Day Butterfly Center, bottom.

friends to pass the day with. As well, parasites and predators are eliminated, and life is good. And they serve as a valuable educational tool. Once a child is exposed to a live butterfly on the wing, they will never look at nature in the same light again. A visit to a facility such as the Day Butterfly Center should be required of everyone. If you leave without a tear in your eye, you need to go back in for a few more minutes. They are tears of joy from witnessing the inner sanctum of grace and beauty.

If you visit the Day Butterfly Center, go to the restaurant at the top of the hill and treat yourself to a muscadine ice cream. My view of heaven would be cool drops of muscadine ice cream delivered to me on the wings of butterflies.

DONNER PASS

One of the most unlikely places in the United States to have a butterfly farm is Donner Pass, California, though it was the site of the first butterfly farm in the country. And the roots of American butterfly farming began there with a young lady's desire to go to college.

Newly emerged butterflies delight all ages

In 1911, not many young ladies were attending college, but that did not hold back Ximena McGlashan. At that time, most families could not afford the tuition, but that did not stop her either. Nor did living in one of the most challenging places for a butterfly farm. Miss McGlashan had a dream. With assistance from her father Charles, she devised a solution. They decided to raise butterflies to pay for college.

Donner Pass is near the town of Truckee, in California's Sierra Nevada Mountains. It's an area that has formidable winter weather. Overnight accumulations of six or more feet of snow are routine for area residents. The snows come early in autumn and leave late in the spring. Named for the Donner Party, a 19th century pioneering expedition headed westward, the snowbound pass blocked the party's westward movement for an entire winter and led to one of the most gruesome tales of human misery in the Old West.

The irony seems so perfect: raising the most delicate of all creatures in a place with such a savage past. This is exactly what Ximena and her father did. In fact, they did so well that she was able to attend college and achieve her dream. And that dream continues with the McGlashan Butterfly Foundation in Truckee, which awards scholarships and grants to Tahoe/Truckee area students for the study of entomology.

HAWAII

Lush vegetation, fertile soil, and a climate to kill for, Hawaii lacks only one thing in abundance: Butterflies. It has everything all the butterfly "hot beds" have. The problem with Hawaii is that it is stuck in the middle of the Pacific Ocean, and butterflies just cannot seem to make it out there on their own. Actually, only the King Kamehameha and Blackburn's Blue are native to Hawaii. Just like many of Hawaii's residents, the other fifteen butterfly species are tourists that never went home. Nonetheless, it seems a shame in such a glorious setting that only seventeen species of butterflies exist.

Some species will only exist at certain elevations and will not be found a mile away. Monarchs, on the other hand, can be found everywhere. Their host plant, the crown flower milkweed, is prevalent and grows to the size of

Views of Kokee State Park in Hawaii where the Cabbage White has made it from Quebec to Kauai in less than a hundred years.

apple trees. Stand near any orchid tree, and you will quickly be surrounded by nectaring Monarchs. Mating takes place all year, so every milkweed plant is covered with larvae.

On the island of Hawaii there exists a race of white Monarchs, a subspecies of their familiar orange-and-black relative. For reasons unknown, they have developed into a white, black-veined race.

But the most noteworthy butterfly I discovered on the Hawaiian Islands is the everyday Cabbage White. Not the most beautiful of all the butterflies, it is the most persistent. The Cabbage White was first imported to Quebec in 1860. Not caring for the cold Canadian winters, populations quickly spread to the United States. Because of its fondness for garden vegetables, the Cabbage White overtook the country in a few decades and can now be found in every state including Alaska.

I do not know if I was surprised or satisfied with my last encounter with this Hawaiian White. We were far above the spectacular Waimea Canyon at Kokee State Park. We were about to embark on a ten-mile hike, far into the sacred Alaka'i Swamp to photograph *Eupithecia orichloris,* the Green Sphinx Moth. As I prepared for the magical pilgrimage, a Cabbage White alighted next to me. It made me think that for all the preparation and planning it took for me to get this far, to this little butterfly it was just another day in the park.

Bunchberries may be the only nectar source for the White-banded Admiral at the summit of Mt. Washington, above.

I've watched so many Whites flit across my garden, I just did not expect a visit from one at 4,000 feet.

MOUNT WASHINGTON, NEW HAMPSHIRE

Go about a mile or so past the tree line and the butterflies are having a ball. Granite outcrops, little vegetation, and the worst weather in the world is not the place for a butterfly to call home. But that is the environment the White-banded Admiral loves. Mount Washington is noted worldwide as having the worst weather ever recorded. For half the year winds are at hurricane force (winds of 230 miles an hour have been recorded). The other half of the year just isn't nice.

Anyone visiting Mount Washington just has to fall in love with its grandeur and the vistas from the summit, which are almost religious when the fog lifts. As we journeyed to the top we saw a Monarch leisurely glide past our windshield at 4,500 feet. A great sight to be sure.

After reaching the summit and snapping back to reality from the view, I thought the only thing that could make this experience any better would be to wish on a butterfly and release it to the Great Spirit. And the Great One was listening. There in front of me sat a beautiful White-banded Admiral, perched and waiting to assist me in my wish. What a wonderful gift at 6,300 feet.

The weather conditions at Mount Washington are not the White-banded Admiral's only hurdles. It has nothing to nectar from except a few bunchberry blooms, which take up to twenty-five years before they produce their first flower. Then up pulls a vanload of tourists, and they trample it back down for another quarter of a century.

But despite the encroachment of humans, both butterflies and bunchberries manage to survive. It warms the heart to know that two of the most delicate creatures in the world, in defiance of everything nature can hurl at them, survive.

FIELDS OF SAINT MATTHEW

Of all the places I've been, the one closest to my heart will always be the Fields of Saint Matthew in Weatherly, Pennsylvania. Not far from my home, these sacred fields were nestled comfortably in a rich valley. On summer days, you once could stand at the edge of the patch-work meadows and witness hundreds of butterflies simultaneously on the wing.

When friends would visit from around the world, they were always treated to an excursion to the Fields of Saint Matthew. It was wonderful to watch the expressions on their faces as they watched Tigers criss-crossing with Spicebushes that were trying to avoid the Frits. Pipevines? Why they're right over there next to the Buckeyes and Painted Ladies. All were amazed by the abundance of butterflies in the valley.

One Christmas morning we decided to pay a short visit to the cradle of my lepidoteran education and wish seasons greetings to Saint Matthew, only to learn that the marvelous Fields of Saint Matthew would be no more. The fields had been mowed to ground level, surely destroying any egg, chrysalis, or caterpillar seeking a refuge from winter. As with many butterfly habitats, the whole valley had been marked off for a housing development. The precious fields in Weatherly can now only live in my mind's eye.

Butterflies are abundant in a
flower-rich meadow, above.

SANIBEL ISLAND, FLORIDA

Located on Florida's beautiful gulf coast, Sanibel Island is a paradise close by. Just over the causeway from Fort Meyers, it requires a visit from anyone in the area. It has long been promoted as a shell collector's paradise, and it justly deserves the reputation. However, that is only one of the many things that makes Sanibel special.

While on the island, I suggest you walk the path from the lighthouse to the parking lot. Here you can watch the Zebra Longwings dance and play. The Gulf Fritillaries seem too busy to notice anyone as they search for lunch. Julia should be down the beach shortly. She always flies by on sunny days. Not only are Sanibel and her sister island Captiva rich with Florida butterflies, but unexpected treasures arrive on every breeze. When traveling on these two jewels, you must always keep your eyes open. It is not unusual to encounter species that drifted in from Mexico. A change in the wind pattern, and you may be introduced to a visitor from the Caribbean. Many species may be viewed only in this section of the gulf.

The island also offers great numbers and varieties of birds to watch in the tropical flora. Tropical strays abound in the avian sector, also. If birds are not to your liking, just plop yourself down on the spectacular beach. If you hold still for a few moments you will be able to watch the dolphins dance. They come very close to shore, and do not mind staying in waist-deep water. They actually enjoy riding along with windsurfers, and are always eager to play.

With the dolphins gone, and the birds away, it is time to head back to the lighthouse path. It is just as much fun watching the Tropical Buckeyes chasing the Ruddy Dagger Wings, while paddling through the "Ding Darling Preserve." Now was that a White Peacock landing on the Lantana?

Julia (top) and the White Peacock (bottom) are regulars along the trail on Sanibel Island.

Abilene Zoological Society   P.O. Box 60, Abilene, TX 79609

American Museum of Natural History   79th Street and Central Park West, New York, NY 10024

John Ball Zoological Garden   201 Market Street, Grand Rapids, MI 49503

Binder Park Zoo   7400 Division Street, Battle Creek, MI 49017

Birmingham Zoo Insectarium   2630 Cahaba Road, Birmingham, AL 35223

Butterfly Emporium   Dollywood, Pigeon Forge, TN

Butterfly Pavilion and Insect Center   6252 West 104th Street, Westminster, CO 80020

The Butterfly Place   Papillon Park, 120 Tyngsboro Road, Westford, MA 01885

Butterfly World   P.O. Box 36, Coombs, British Columbia, V0R 1M0

Cape May Bird Observatory   P.O. Box 3, Cape May Point, NJ 08212

Cincinnati Zoo Insectarium   3400 Vine Street, Cincinnati, OH 45220

The Cockerell Butterfly Center   One Herman Circle Drive, Houston, TX 77030

Cushing Butterfly Farm   1512 Jenny Lane, Richmond, TX

The Day Butterfly Center   Callaway Gardens, Pine Mountain, GA 31822-2000

Detroit Zoological Park   8450 W. 10 Mile Road, Royal Oak, MI 48068

Doorly Zoo   3701 S. 10th Street, Omaha, NE 68107

Fort Worth Zoological Insectarium   2727 Zoological Park Drive, Fort Worth, TX 76110

Greater Los Angeles Zoo   5333 Zoo Drive, Los Angeles, CA 90027-1498

Kalamazoo Nature Center   7000 N. Westnedge Avenue, Kalamazoo, MI 49004-0127

Mackinac Island Butterfly House   Sawyers Greenhouse, 1308 McGaulpin, Mackinac Island, MI 49757

Magic Wings, Museum of Life and Science   443 Murray Avenue, Durham, NC 27704

Marine World Africa-USA   Marine World Parkway, Vallejo, CA 94589

Michigan State University Butterfly House   Department of Entomology, East Lansing, MI

Moody Gardens   Hope Boulevard, Houston, TX

Museum of Science and Industry   4801 E. Fowler Avenue, Tampa, FL

Musser's Butterfly Farm   RR#7, 13200 Fulton Road, Sidney, OH 45365

National Zoological Park   3000 Connecticut Avenue NW , Washington, DC 20008

Newport Butterfly Farm   594 Aquidneck Avenue, Middleton, RI 02842

Niagara Parks Butterfly Conservatory   P.O. Box 150, Niagara Falls, Ontario

Rocky Mountain Butterfly Center   6252 W. 104th Avenue, Westminster, CO

Saginaw Children's Zoo   1435 S. Washington, Saginaw, MI 48601

St. Louis Zoological Park   Forest Park, St. Louis, MO 63110

San Antonio Zoological Garden   3903 North St. Mary's, San Antonio, TX 78212

San Diego Wild Animal Park   15500 San Pasqual Valley Road, Escondido, CA 92027-9614

San Francisco Zoological Society Insect Zoo   Zoo Road, San Francisco, CA 94132

Smithsonian Insect Zoo   National Museum of Natural History,_____

Sonoran Anthropod Studies, Inc. (SASI) Insect Zoo   2437 North Stone Avenue, Tucson, AZ 85703

Washington Park Zoo   4001 SW Canyon Road, Portland, OR 97221

Yeager Butterfly Farm   570 William Drive, Pearsall, TX 78061

Zilker Botanical Gardens   Barton Spring Road, Austin, TX

GALLERY OF GARDEN BUTTERFLIES

Papilio zelicaon

Anise Swallowtail

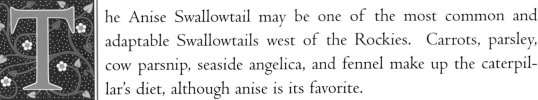

he Anise Swallowtail may be one of the most common and adaptable Swallowtails west of the Rockies. Carrots, parsley, cow parsnip, seaside angelica, and fennel make up the caterpillar's diet, although anise is its favorite.

The Anise Swallowtail lays its cream-colored eggs individually. The caterpillars are usually green or greenish-blue and have black vertical stripes with yellow or orange dots. Pupa can vary from light brown to black. Regardless of color, they all rely on a mid-dorsal band to suspend from during hibernation, attaching to a vertical support much like a telephone lineman girds to a telephone pole.

The Anise is a moderate-sized Swallowtail, with the male and female looking much the same. Yellow dashes line the outside margin of both wings. Through the center of the wings is a row of bold yellow spots that meet just above a blue blush which halos two orange spots with black centers — all set on a black background. From below, they are even more exquisite, showcasing a rich mosaic of yellow, blue, and orange.

All Swallowtails perform a ritual called "hill-topping," looking for mates from the top of a mound or rise. On the wing, the male can be distinguished from the female by its bobbing flight, wherein males investigate every chance to mate or to chase off intruders. Soon after mating, the females begin laying eggs.

In southern California, the adult Anise can be found year-round. They range from sea level to just above the tree line, although Anise have been recorded at elevations up to 14,000 feet.

Anise Swallowtails favor nectar plants such as butterfly bush, lantana, and zinnia and can be found from the sage deserts to city lots.

Range: *West of the Rocky Mountains. Mexico to the maritime Northwest.*

Attracted to:
butterfly bush, lantana, zinnia, anise, fennel, lavendar, parsley, yarrow, carrots, cow parsnip and seaside angelica

Papilio polyxenes

Eastern Black Swallowtail

he high point of summer is going out to my favorite fields and beholding a sight that few are privileged to see. On a warm summer day any number of fields will have dozens and sometimes hundreds of Black Swallowtails glissading over them. Turn around to view another field, and you will be rewarded with more flying ebony jewels.

Also called the Parsnip or Black Swallowtail, the sexes of this species are a little easier to tell apart than the closely related Anise. The Eastern Black Swallowtail female has more blue on the hindwing than does the male. Rows of yellow spots on the forewing and hindwings of the male help to set it apart from the female. In the field they can both be distinguished from the Pipevine by its lazier flight pattern. The Eastern Black Swallowtail prefers to flit from plant to plant, never quite stopping its wings while it feeds.

The cream-colored or yellow eggs can be found on Queen Anne's lace, parsley, carrots, and even Texas turpentine. Because of their fondness for garden plants such as celery and dill, adult Eastern Black Swallowtails visit gardens.

Newly emerged caterpillars are black with a white saddle. They soon develop greenish-black vertical stripe with yellow dots. As with the other Swallowtails, the caterpillars have the orange osmeterium that delivers a horrible odor to would-be predators, which works amazingly well. There can be two or three broods, depending on the latitude. The chrysalis can vary from green to brown. The color of the pupa can be affected by the time of year or the surface that it forms on. Rough surfaces usually produce a brown chrysalis, while smooth surfaces yield a green-colored chrysalis.

Male Eastern Black Swallowtails prefer to post and patrol for females. The Eastern Black Swallowtail's flight pattern is short and erratic. Try to catch one, and it is a straight bee-line to the next field or garden.

Range: *Common east of the Rockies, from Canada to Mexico.*

ATTRACTED TO:
celery, dill, fennel, carrots, caraway, lavendar, parsley, rue, yarrow, parsley, Queen Anne's lace and Texas turpentine

Papilio cresphontes

GIANT SWALLOWTAIL

he giant gets its name for good reason: It is huge. Finding your first Giant caterpillar can be quite an experience. It resembles a six-inch piece of bird dung. Its mottled brown body is offset by a saddle of cream, buff body patches, and a red osmeterium. The larva can usually be found near various citrus trees to which it can do considerable damage. Citrus growers refer to it as the Orange Dog because of its appetite for their crops. It is sometimes considered a pest and has been the target of insecticide spraying.

The yellow, orange, or sometimes green eggs, are laid on the tips of citrus leaves. A female may deposit up to 500 in her life. The larvae will also feed on prickly ash, hoptree, and even rue in the northern part of their range. The resulting chrysalis is grayish-brown. It flies year-round in the South, where it is multi-brooded. In the northern edges of its range it may only have two broods per season.

The nearly six-inch black wings are complemented with beautiful rows of yellow spots. One row seems to connect the wingtips as it crosses the body, while the other row plays down the wing margins. The underside is in perfect contrast — bright yellow with black trim. The enormous wings are capable of long, leisurely flights. Giant Swallowtails seem to prefer gliding rather than flapping. The males prefer to patrol for females and are regular visitors to puddle clubs.

Giant Swallowtails are more at home in citrus groves, glades, and edges, but they will come to gardens. The adults can be found nectaring at orange blossoms, lantana, and honeysuckle.

The largest of all the North American Swallowtails, the Giant's enormous wings can carry it as far north as Canada and as far south as the Caribbean.

Range: *Gulf states, through the Midwest to the Great Lakes and the Northeast.*

ATTRACTED TO:
orange blossoms, lantana,
honeysuckle, rue,
prickly ash and hoptree

Papilio palamedes

PALAMEDES SWALLOWTAIL

The *Great Swamp Thing* may be a more appropriate name for this brownish-black beauty. More common in the South, Palamedes Swallowtail can be easily recognized by its lazy flight. It prefers swampy areas, where it can be found nectaring from pickerelweed. Palamedes does match the Giant Swallowtail in size. The yellow spots of Palamedes are not as large as the Giant's, but run parallel across both wings. On the Giant, the yellow spots converge into one row that ends at the wingtip.

Palamedes Swallowtail's yellow-green eggs can be found on magnolia, bay, or sassafras. The caterpillars resemble those of the spicebush, having the typical set of false eyespots. The larvae like to rest on silk mat in the center of a bowed leaf. They will winter either as a larva or as a greenish-patterned chrysalis. In the Deep South there may be three broods, but in most cases only two.

The adult Palamedes Swallowtail can be of quite an impressive size, reaching up to five and one-half inches. Appearing brownish-black from above, they have two rows of yellow spots. The first row parallels the outside margin of both wings. The inner row begins as yellow spots on the forewing and blends to a yellow bar on the hindwing. The underside is a wonderful mix of orange zigzags, blue crescents, and creamy-colored spots on a black background. Their black bodies are lined with lateral yellow stripes.

Male Palamedes Swallowtails can be found patrolling wooded areas or at puddle clubs. There are occasions when adults will rest communally. In some regions, Palamedes is referred to as the Laurel Swallowtail because of its fondness for that shrubbery. More at home in the shadier section of a garden, they can also be found nectaring from phlox, azaleas, and loosestrife.

Range: *Wetlands from Maryland to Missouri and south to the Gulf of Mexico.*

ATTRACTED TO:
*phlox, azaleas, loosestrife,
sassafras, pickerelweed,
magnolia and bay*

Battus philenor

Pipevine Swallowtail

In the Philippines, a black butterfly is a sign of bad luck. This is especially true if you happen to be an insect-eating vertebrate. The larvae of the Pipevine Swallowtail consumes wild ginger, Dutchman's pipe, and knotweeds, which renders them very distasteful, and sometimes deadly to birds. This defense mechanism works so well that it is copied by many other butterflies. The color pattern of the Pipevine Swallowtail is a symphony of blues and blacks.

More common in the southern United States, the adults can be found nectaring at honeysuckle, orchids, and azalea. The females are less colorful, but larger whitish spots along the margin of the forewing assist in distinguishing them from the males. Often called the Blue Swallowtail, the hindwings of the male Pipevine Swallowtail can be metallic blue or green. If the colorful announcement of "trouble ahead" is not enough, there are glands on the abdomen that emit an acidic odor when squeezed.

The Pipevine is one of the few butterflies that lays its eggs in clusters. The orange eggs can be found in numbers from one to twenty on pipevines or snakeroot. The caterpillars are gregarious and quite formidable looking. The dark purplish-brown larva has two gruesome filaments projecting forward. Eventually the caterpillar will become a tan or green chrysalis suspended by a girdle filament. There are two broods in the North and three in the South.

When the Pipevine begins to emerge in the spring, it's a thing of real beauty. Sacramento, California, in the spring is noted for Pipevines.

To consider the sight of a black butterfly a sign of bad luck is an unfortunate custom. In today's environment we are lucky to see any at all. So any day that we see butterflies is a lucky day indeed.

Range: *Throughout the United States with exception of the northern tier of the Rockies.*

Attracted to:
honeysuckle, orchids, azalea, wild ginger, Dutchman's pipe, knotweed, pipevine and snakeroot

Papilio troilus

Spicebush Swallowtail

alk the wooded edges of any forest and you may get to see the Spicebush Swallowtail. One most unforgettable experiences happened to me on an early autumn day. As I walked a logging road, I spotted a large black butterfly bobbing about the ground, alighting repeatedly on the same small area. I approached slowly to avoid frightening it away. It was a male Spicebush Swallowtail attempting to chase a discarded shotgun shell from its territory. The green plastic of the spent shell was enough to convince the Spicebush that his mating territory was in jeopardy by another male.

Often called the Green or Green-clouded butterfly, the males have a greenish tint to their hindwings; the females sport a bluish hue. Underneath they are black, with wonderful orange-red spots on the hindwing.

As per its namesake, the eggs of the Spicebush are usually found on spicebush. Sometimes sassafras or bays will be used. The pale green eggs give rise to a dark green caterpillar. Near its head it also has the typical orange and black eyespots of Swallowtail larvae. When not feeding, they favor hiding in drawn-up leaves. There are two broods in the North and three in the South. The chrysalis can be either green or bark-colored. Early-season chrysalis tend to be green, and later ones brown. The coloration is said to be affected by the light at different times of year. Adults emerging in the spring seem to be smaller than those of the later season. They have a rapid and direct flight, and the males prefer to patrol woodland edges.

Spicebushes can't pass up a Joy-Pye weed when it is in bloom. They will also nectar at lantana, jewelweed, and honeysuckle. Lovers of wooded areas, they are just at home in the garden. As with all large, black Swallowtails, they attempt to trick predators into thinking that they may be the distasteful Pipevine.

Range: *North America from Canada to Florida and west to the Rockies.*

Attracted to:
lantana, jewelweed, honeysuckle, sassafras, spicebush or bays

Papilio glaucus (Eastern)
Papilio rutulus (Western)

TIGER SWALLOWTAIL

Every area of the country has its own variation of the Tiger Swallowtail. This bright yellow butterfly with black tiger stripes can be found throughout the eastern United States and Canada. If you have lilacs in your garden, you most certainly will have Tigers.

The striking yellow and black against the lavender blooms is perfect harmony. Western Tigers prefer moist areas with willows and poplar. The Two-tailed Tiger west of the Rockies range from Texas to Montana and from California to Oregon. To make things more interesting still, in parts of Arizona lives the Three-tailed Tiger. And to complicate things even more, the females are dimorphic. The female can be black or dark brown above, but the tiger striping is still visible on the underside of the forewings. The Eastern Tiger Swallowtail can be quite common east of the Rockies. Its large yellow wings make it obvious in garden or field. Northeastern Swallowtails may be smaller and paler than those of those in the South.

The yellow-green eggs are deposited on willow, birch, tulips, and cherries. Newly hatched caterpillars look like brown and white bird droppings. As it grows older it will become a smooth green larva with orange eyespots and a yellow back band. The larvae are hard to locate because of their preference for feeding in treetops. They are content to rest in a rolled leaf nest when not feeding. Just prior to changing into a chrysalis, the caterpillar may become brownish. Chrysalides may be green or brown, but they always suspend from a twig.

The male Tiger is very attracted to puddling. The females can be distinguished by the abundance of blue on the upper surface of the hindwing. The strong flight pattern allows this yellow giant to be a regular visitor to gardens. The adults are quite fond of buddleia, honeysuckle, bee balm, and sunflowers.

Range: *Throughout the United States east of the Rockies and into the Canadian Maritimes, allowing the Tiger to sometimes reach the southern tip of Alaska.*

ATTRACTED TO:
buddleia, honeysuckle, bee balm, sunflowers, lilacs, willow, birch, tulips and cherries

Eurytides marcellus

Zebra Swallowtail

This delicate-looking Swallowtail is North America's only representative of the Kite Swallowtails, named for their triangle-shaped wings and long tail. There cannot be an afternoon more pleasurable than watching Zebras. And the area of choice is the shores of the Chesapeake Bay. A Zebra's day starts with a wake-up drink at the bay edge, then on to nectar. Perhaps a little socializing and some mating afterwards. If the day should heat up, they will seek sanctuary in the cool, shaded treetops.

If you have pawpaw, you'll probably have Zebra Swallowtails visiting them, for they are the host plant of choice. Along the banks of the Potomac there is a lot of pawpaw, which has led some to think that there may be too many Zebras in the area. Having too many butterflies would be like winning too much money in the lottery.

The Zebra Swallowtail's green egg will be found only on pawpaw. The green caterpillar has one black band across the back and several yellow bands across its length. The green or brown chrysalis will be stockier than those of other Swallowtails. The rotund little barrel of emerald looks like it may explode.

Adults that emerge earlier in the season are smaller, paler, and have shorter tails than do the later ones, which can be over an inch long. The underside of the hindwing has a brilliant red stripe that flashes wonderfully because of the Zebra's bat-like wing flap. The red dots visible from the upper surface remind us of the Native American legend: The red dots symbolize the blood that will be shed by anyone who harms this delicate creature. Triangular wings, beautiful colors, and gorgeous, long tails make the Zebra Swallowtail a natural masterpiece of physical art.

Although it prefers wooded areas and wet spots, it will reluctantly visit suburban neighborhoods.

Range: *The Great Lakes to Florida and along the Gulf to the Great Plains.*

ATTRACTED TO:
pawpaw

Vanessa virginiensis

American Painted Lady

This "Virginia Lady," as she is known in some parts, has a fondness for heliotrope. If she cannot find any, she will hunt for zinnia or yarrow. Perhaps that is why she is also known as the Hunter's Butterfly.

The color pattern of the American Painted Lady is similar to that of its cousin, the Painted Lady — orange and black in no particular order. The key distinguishing characteristic of the American Painted Lady is the blush of pinkish-rose on the mid-forewing.

The most obvious field mark that sets the American Painted Lady apart from her cousin, the Painted Lady, are the two large blue eyespots on the underside of the hindwing. The Painted Lady sports four eyespots while the West Coast Lady has five. The West Coast Lady also has an orange bar on the forewing as opposed to the pink of the Hunter.

The yellowish-green eggs of the American Painted Lady are usually deposited on the leaves of everlasting and on daisies. The black caterpillar, the larval stage of this butterfly, has yellow cross bands with red and white spots between them. The larva may pupate in its gold-speckled, brown chrysalis. Although the American Painted Lady can survive colder temperatures than its cousins, it still has only two broods in the North, but more in the South.

The American Painted Lady is found throughout the United States, where its numbers are usually greater in the East than in the West.

With its fondness for garden flowers, the American Painted Lady is a regular visitor to yards and open places. Comfortable in various habitats, the American Painted Lady does not migrate to the extent that her relatives do.

Range: *Canada to Central America and from the East Coast to the West Coast of the United States.*

ATTRACTED TO:
mallow, borage, burdock, heliotrope, zinnia, yarrow, daisies and everlasting

Speyeriis aphrodite

APHRODITE FRITILLARY

he Goddess of love, Aphrodite is beautiful and beguiling. The mystery: Is she really the temptress or the Great Spangled, a species that looks very similar? Clues are present to help us. Aphrodite is slightly smaller, with a wingspan of less than three and a half inches. The Great Spangled measures nearly four inches across. The cream-colored band on the hindwing is small and its shading is dark on her highness Aphrodite. On her counterpart, the Great Spangled, the creamy band is quite large and occupies most of the wing surface.

A common practice of all Fritillaries is the depositing of eggs near the site where violets will emerge the following year. By the time the female is ready to lay her eggs, the violets have bloomed and died. The females smell the dormant roots, and the scent becomes the signal for where to place the ovum.

Aphrodite's cream-colored egg will take on a violet nuance just prior to emergence. Aphrodite's spiny, brownish-black caterpillar eagerly devours the springtime violet leaves. The larva passes the winter before pupating, a practice of most Fritillaries. The chrysalis is brownish-black near the head, yellowish-brown at the wings, and grayish-white at the abdomen. The blend of hues and shades is a camouflage of sorts that helps Aphrodite elude predators.

The orange and black adults are not as dark toward the body as are the Great Spangled. Aphrodite's darker shading appears to radiate outward from the body. On the Great Spangled, the shading may cover the entire upper wing.

Although its flight period is later than the other Fritillaries, Aphrodite makes up for lost time by being a quicker flyer. Aphrodite and the Great Spangled have ranges that overlap and they share much of the same environment.

Range: *The northern tier of the United States, from the Rocky Mountain eastern front to Maine.*

ATTRACTED TO:
*thistle, dogbane
and violet leaves*

Junonia coenia

BUCKEYE

The Buckeye is not easily confused with any other North American butterfly. The large eyespots on the upper side of the wings startle man and beast alike. Wing colors vary from tawny to brown. Each forewing has two short red bars at the center, flanked by a white stripe that intersects with the forewing eyespot. The hindwing has two eyespots resting on a bar of orange that arches through its center. The entire surface is highlighted with iridescent colors. When viewed under the correct lighting, it is a stunning halo of infinite hues. Underneath, the forewing is a lighter version of the top surface. The hindwing is a mottled combination of tan and reddish brown. The forewing eyespot is visible from the underside, but those of the hindwing are vague.

The squat, dark-green egg is deposited on plantain, stonecrop, and snapdragon as well as many other garden flowers. The spiny black caterpillar has two rows of orange spots along the back and two rows along the sides. Its branched spines protrude from blue bases. The chrysalis can range from tan to mottled brown, but are generally sprinkled with cream-colored flecks. The Buckeye has several broods per year in the South, whereas only two in the North.

Unable to withstand winter in the North, the Buckeye migrates south in the fall. During autumn along the East Coast, the number of Buckeyes rivals the number of Monarchs heading south.

Buckeye males are not as energetic as their cousins. Once a male locates a breeding territory, he prefers to conserve his energy and intercept passing ladies.

Buckeyes are as fond of garden flowers as they are of mud puddles, where they can be found basking with wings spread wide.

Inspect a Buckeye and see how colorful a butterfly can be.

Range: *Throughout the United States, with the exception of the Pacific Northwest.*

ATTRACTED TO:
*plantain, stonecrop,
snapdragon and
garden flowers*

Cercyonis pegala

COMMON WOOD NYMPH

es, the woods are filled with elfins and nymphs. And every morning at sunrise, they do a magical dance throughout the woodlands as they search for sweets. Actually, there are butterflies called Elfins, which are small and brown, and Nymphs, which are larger and eyed.

You won't soon forget the first large Wood Nymph you see. The woodsy-brown wings can span almost three inches. The striking yellow patch on the forewing has two black eyespots with powder blue pupils. It is hard to find a Wood Nymph with its wings apart, because it keeps the eyes a secret. The coffee-brown hindwing has only two black dots with light blue centers. Blending well with the bark of trees, the busy brown pattern of the underside camouflages its bearer well.

This species causes a lot of confusion because of its geographic color variations. In different parts of the country it is even called by different names, such as Blue-eyed Grayling or Goggle Eyes. By any name it is still quite a sight.

Females place their squat yellow eggs near or on grasses. Soon the yellowish-green caterpillar emerges. Covered with short, fuzzy hair, the larva has four yellow stripes running from the head to two red points at the rear. It overwinters shortly after hatching and waits until the following spring to produce a green chrysalis. Emerging between June and September, the Wood Nymph produces only one brood per year. The females are usually larger than the males, but southeastern Wood Nymphs are bigger than their cousins, regardless of sex.

The Wood Nymph may not be the fleetest of wing, but it is a skilled and artful dodger accustomed to weaving through trees and grasses. An occasional visitor to the garden with an appreciation for flowers, it still harbors a sweet tooth for rotting fruit.

Range: *Throughout the United States except the extreme southwest and the southern tip of Florida.*

ATTRACTED TO:
*rotting fruit and
garden flowers*

Speyeria cybele

GREAT SPANGLED FRITILLARY

he Great Spangled was named for a French jewelry box. *Vol bijou* seems to be a perfect name for this insect, with its flashes of silver and gold. The underside of this Fritillary's orange and black wings are inlaid with circles of silver, making them seem bejeweled.

In the scheme of butterfly life, the Fritillaries seem to have trouble with their timing. After mating in July, the female lays her eggs in August or September. Most "Frits" only use members of the Viola family as host plants. The tan egg is laid in the vicinity of violets, which will not be consumed for several months. In a few days the emerging larva will eat its shell and then hibernate for winter. The following spring, as temperatures begin to climb, it will awake to fresh violet leaves to eat. The ebony larvae are covered with black-tipped orange spines.

When other butterflies are starting a second brood, the nocturnal-feeding fritillary caterpillar is starting to form its chrysalis. The pupa is a blend of browns, sometimes with a reddish tinge. By June they are ready to emerge into the large burnt orange and black masters of the skies. Its strong flight enables the Great Spangled to enjoy a wide range that encompasses most of the U.S.

The upper wings are dark umber near the centers, lightening to orange approaching the margins. All four wings are flecked with black zigzags, chevrons, and dots. The underside of the forewings are creamy orange with black zigzags, but the hindwings are reddish brown with large silver spots. An excellent field mark is the wide cream band paralleling the brown wing margin of the underside.

The Great Spangled is fond of thistle, composites, and dung, and will come to the garden.

Range: *Throughout the U.S., except for the Gulf states and southern California.*

ATTRACTED TO:
*violet leaves, thistle,
composites and dung*

Limenitis lorquini

Lorquin's Admiral

ierre Lorquin should be proud to have such a striking example of Lepidoptera bearing his name. The French collector was most excited to send his *vol bijou* back to 19th century Europe.

Lorquin's Admiral is abundant in the Western parks and river bottoms. The willows and poplars that it needs grow well in the West's mid-elevations. Wherever the host plants thrive, so will this Admiral. They can even be found in some seemingly isolated areas such as Aspen Valley, in Yosemite, or in the canyons of the Rockies.

The Admiral's orange-tipped brown wings makes it quite noticeable against its favored Upper Sonoran landscape. All the Admirals have white or cream-colored bars transversing the center of both wings, but Lorquin's is the only one with tangerine-colored tips. Underneath there is a zigzag pattern of alternating rows of brick-red, black, and white over-laying an orange base. The typical cream-colored midwing bars of the Admiral are quite evident when the wings are folded.

Leaf tips seem to be the chosen site for the silvery-pale-green ovum. The dark, young offspring have white saddles on their backs, but for only a short time. They eventually turn yellowish brown or olive, with light side stripes and a white back patch. Plume-like bristles protrude from behind the head. The half-grown larvae spend the winters hibernating in a rolled leaf. When the chrysalis is finally formed, it is a swirl of purple, gray, and olive tones. The Northwest is limited to only one brood, but in California they are graced with two. Lorquin's Admiral does not exist elsewhere in the U.S.

Males are territorial against all odds. It is not unusual to see a Lorquin's Admiral dive-bombing birds or chastising a cat that wandered into the wrong place. As soon as the inter-loper is driven off, the Admiral resumes its perch and awaits females.

Range: *From the Baja Peninsula to British Columbia and east to Nevada and Idaho.*

Attracted to:
willows and poplars

Boloria bellona

Meadow Fritillary

long roadsides and in damp meadows it is often easy to see smaller versions of the Fritillaries. The Meadow Fritillaries come in two models: the Eastern and Western. It is only the name that they share, since their tastes are very different. The Easterns fancy the northern and central sections of the country, while the Westerns find the Northwest to their liking. The Eastern is usually referred to simply as the Meadow Fritillary. It is more abundant and enjoys a much larger range than its Western relative.

The Meadow Fritillary's white egg yields a purplish-black caterpillar that is covered with brown, branching spines. Along the length of the back will be dark chevrons, and dashes lining the side. Typically it will eat violets until chrysalis time. The pupae are brown to yellowish-brown, with gold markings. There is more of a yellowish hue near the abdomen area than overall.

The Meadow Fritillary's wings are more angulated than those of the larger Fritillaries. However, the brownish-orange wings with black dashes and dots are still representative of the species. Unlike its larger cousins, this Fritillary is a rich combination of colors. The lack of silvery spots underneath is compensated for by swirling purples, grays, and browns. The black zigzag pattern will also be noticeable on the underside of the forewing.

The larva of the Western is gray, with dorsal lines and reddish side stripes. The spines are mostly red, which become black near its black head. The chrysalis is mottled with browns and white toward the midsection. The adults are similar but the Western Meadows have rounder wingtips than the Easterns. They all tend to fly in a rapid zigzag pattern while staying low to the ground. Males can usually be found searching wet areas for potential mates.

Range: *The Eastern Meadow Fritillary resides in the northeastern and north-central sections of the country. The Western Meadow Fritillary occupies the northwestern corner of the U.S.*

ATTRACTED TO:
violet leaves

Nymphalis milberti

MILBERT'S TORTOISE SHELL

hen at rest, these butterflies expose the intricate turtle-shell patterns of their underwings. This is an excellent example of camouflage used in combination with the stunning colors of the upper wings. A predator could nearly step on this clever rascal, not seeing it for the surroundings. Then, at the last moment, there is a dazzling display of confusing colors. As quickly as it flashes, it is gone, leaving the predator startled.

Females carefully search for nettles on which to lay large clusters of their pale green eggs. The caterpillars live together for a short period in a silken nest. Eventually they separate and live solitary lives inside rolled leaves. There is some variation of colors between siblings, but all have black, branched spines. Most of the larvae are black above and covered with white and orange dots. The sides appear yellowish-green, due to the thin lateral lines blending together. The pupal coloration is variable, running from gray to golden green or nearly black. The chrysalis is a bit more slender and a bit longer than those of other members in this group. It is the adult that hibernates in the winter, not the pupa.

The inner area of the upper wings of Milbert's Tortoise Shell are a rich coffee-without-cream color. A wide bar of yellow changing to orange parallels the outer wing margins. Along the forewing margins are slight white dashes; those lining the hind wing are blue. There is also a faint white smudge near the apex of the forewings. Between the smudges and the body are two small orange blazes. Below is a mixture of dark earth tones that create the deceptive pattern.

A woodsy setting is more to the liking of Milbert's, but it is versatile and can be found in various habitats. The males use stony areas and rock piles as an observatory for spotting passing females rather than patrolling. Conserving their energy in this way may be why they are one of the longer-lived butterflies.

Range: *From Alaska to the nation's midsection and coast to coast.*

ATTRACTED TO:
hop vine and nettles

Danaus plexippus

MONARCH

The Monarch truly deserves its name and is probably one of the most famous butterflies in the world. As an aerialist, it is the sovereign of the skies, completing a feat of migration unique among butterflies.

The sexes can be easily told apart with the use of two distinguishing traits. In the center of the hindwing on the males is a raised black dot. This is the scent pouch, which releases the pheromones that attract the female Monarch. The veins of the female's wings are much bolder than the male's, and in flight appear to be darker orange. On the wing, males seem to be bright orange because their wing veins are thinner.

The ivory-colored eggs will be placed on milkweeds to emerge in three to five days. The caterpillars announce to predators that they are dangerous by way of their warning colors. The white, black, and yellow caterpillars with two thin filaments at each end of the body have ravenous appetites. The inch-long, jade-green chrysalis is studded with gold. Near the top the dots merge into a golden line which nearly encircles it. This is actually how they got their names. American colonists noticed this adornment, which looked much like the crown of their king. After about two weeks, the caterpillars change into adults, becoming perhaps one of the most beautiful creatures in all of nature.

The Monarch is best known for its amazing migration. During autumn, Monarchs fly from Canada to Mexico in six to eight weeks. West Coast Monarchs stay in temperate central California. Then in the spring, the Eastern Monarchs head back north. Monarchs have returned to the same Canadian garden in which they were tagged.

The Monarch is a regular and welcomed guest in gardens. Ask anyone to name a butterfly and you will surely hear the word Monarch.

Range: *Throughout the U.S. (many areas have Monarch subspecies).*

ATTRACTED TO:
milkweeds

Nymphalis antiopa

Mourning Cloak

The exotic Mourning Cloak is unmistakable with its unique coloration. The wings are brownish-maroon, framed with a cream border along the angulated edges. There is a row of blue dots paralleling the cream band, and two creamy yellow dashes at the leading edge of the forewing.

From the underside the wing patterns look like tree bark, with dirty grayish-yellow edges. It is a wonderful example of cryptic camouflage that serves its bearer well. The medley of somber tones allows it to blend into a background of tree bark or earth. The basking adults will hold perfectly still as danger approaches. Then, at the very last moment, the colorful wings snap open, momentarily distracting the assailant as the Mourning Cloak escapes. At rest with folded wings, the Mourning Cloak is nearly impossible to see.

The pale whitish eggs darken considerably prior to hatching. Unlike most other Lepidoptera, the Mourning Cloak lays her eggs in groupings of up to several hundred. The ebony caterpillar has several rows of branching spines between which are red spots that match the legs. Then for extra measure, the whole shebang is sprinkled with white flecks.

The chrysalis of the Mourning Cloak varies from whitish tan to bluish black, with pink-tipped bumps. The hibernating period is passed in the adult stage. As temperatures begin drop, the Mourning Cloak searches for wood piles, loose tree bark, or even the eaves of a house as a winter residence.

The first warm day of spring brings them out to gather nectar from woodpecker drillings and other tree wounds. They are attracted to mud and fruit more than to the garden. But never doubt that the first butterfly seen in the spring is a Mourning Cloak.

Range: *Much of the Northern Hemisphere, from Alaska to South America.*

ATTRACTED TO:
mud, fruit, tree sap

Vanessa cardui

PAINTED LADY

anessa, the Painted Lady, is also known by some aliases. Sometimes she is known as the Thistle butterfly, other times she is called Cosmopolite. The lady has a world-wide reputation from the Arctic to Central America, and on any given day she can be found just about anywhere in the world.

Actually, the Painted Lady is probably the most widespread of all butterflies, and its migratory habits can rival those of the Monarch. The trip is only one-way for this traveler, since it cannot winter in an area where temperatures are severe. From Europe to Africa and Asia to Hawaii, sooner or later Vanessa will be on the scene. Wherever her journeys take her, her favorite meal is thistle.

The color pattern of Vanessa's two-and-a-half-inch wings is orange, black, and white, and not in any order. The black tips of the forewing are dotted with white; the remaining half is a swirl of orange and black. The hindwings are orange with black dots and diamonds set inside the black marginal edge. Underneath, the pattern consists of mottled browns, grays, white, and a wash of rose on the forewing, which is how the Painted Lady got its name.

Early miners in the West — Forty-Niners — required a little relaxation now and then, and would visit the hostesses who were employed by the saloons. These entrepreneurs were referred to by the miners as painted ladies because of their fondness for rouge. After a hard day of working the claims, a Forty-Niner's thoughts would turn to his favorite lady. The wash of pink on the underwing of the Painted Lady reminded him of his favorite lady.

The pale green or yellowish eggs can be found on hollyhock, borage, and pearly everlasting. Painted Lady caterpillars vary greatly in color, as do the branched spines on their backs. There is a broken yellow line down both sides of the abdomen. The chrysalides resemble little pieces of twigs as they hang from their perches. Their brownish hue and twisted shapes are excellent camouflage.

Range: *Worldwide, except for the Arctic.*

ATTRACTED TO:
*borage, burdock,
mallow, thistle, hollyhock,
and pearly everlasting*

Polygonia interrogationis

QUESTION MARK

olygonia interrogationis. Could a name be any more appropriate for a butterfly? On the underside of the hindwing is a silver question mark. This helps distinguish the Question Mark from its cousin the Comma, which sports its punctuation marks likewise. The Anglewings are best known for the jagged or angulated edge of their wings. From above, the three-inch wings are orange spiced with black dots. They are also outlined with a beautiful lavender border. The underside is a gentle mosaic of subtle browns and orange, with a blush of violet. The hindwings terminate into projections that resemble small tails.

The long green eggs, which are laid collectively, will usually be found on elm, hops, or nettles. They may also be stacked vertically. The caterpillar is rusty brown to orange and covered irregularly with white dots. Except for two black branching spines on the head, those on the body are orange. Yellow or orange lines run the length of the body. The grayish-brown chrysalis hangs like a spent leaf, a disguise that keeps it from being devoured by predators. The pupa however, is used only for the transition, since the Question Mark spends the winter as an adult. It is usually on the wing as soon as temperatures allow.

The Question Mark is extremely fond of rotting fruit and will become intoxicated if its dinner is fermented. No one should drink and fly. So as the Question Mark tries to bask off a hangover the morning after, its protective coloration saves it from hungry eyes. Not an eager visitor to the garden, the Question Mark lurks in the shadowy edges of the forest. The males are late risers and do not post for females until the afternoon. Even then they remain on the trunks of trees, waiting for females to approach them.

Range: *From Canada to the Gulf and from the Atlantic to the Rockies.*

ATTRACTED TO:
*nettles, rotting fruit,
elm and hops*

Vanessa atalanta

RED ADMIRAL

his swift flier is easily spotted in the field. The reddish-orange semi-circle pattern on the velvety black wings sets it apart. Worldwide in its distribution, the Red Admiral can be found anywhere in the United States, and it strays as far north as Alaska in the summer. They are attracted to human perspiration and will readily land on someone's shoulder. They are somewhat territorial, too. If your garden is chosen, you will have the privilege of seeing the same faithful guardian assume its post for weeks. The springtime dispersal of adults is said to be followed by a return flight in the fall.

If you have nettles, you'll have Red Admirals. They love nettles, which is also where they lay their eggs. The green eggs soon become black larvae. Their color varies but always in darker tones. The body segments are separated by narrow white stripes. The head may be black, but the body is usually yellow, white, or green. Not to mention the resulting color combinations that arise, complicating matters more — black head and yellow body, brown head and yellow body, or black head and white body.

The larvae live in folded leaves that are lined with silk. Sometimes the Red Admiral may pupate inside. They hibernate and will be on the wing with any warm day. There are two broods in most of the range, but consistently in the South.

When the ship is in port, the Admiral is not opposed to taking a drink. They will nectar from fermented fruit and tree sap as quickly as from flowers. They seem to like getting a bit tipsy, which would account for their erratic flight. Although it is a swift flier, the Red Admiral is not as prone to flying away as are the other butterflies. At certain times they even seem to tolerate humans.

In the past, they were called the Alderman butterfly. Whenever you spot the distinctive red circular pattern against the black background, it means that the Admiral is on deck.

Range: *From the East Coast to Hawaii and from Canada to Central America.*

ATTRACTED TO:
*nettles, hop vine, tree sap
and fermented fruit*

Limenitis arthemis

RED-SPOTTED PURPLE

If you see a patch of black on the top of a tree, it is a Red-spotted Purple. Even the name sounds like a delightful mix of colors. When those perched wings take to the air, you will be treated to a lovely show of brilliant blue iridescence.

The outside margin of the wings are haloed in subtle white dashes. The forewing has a few red dots just inside some of the white ones. Two rows of blue dashes complement the blue bars of the backwing. The underside is reddish-brown, with red spots nearer the body. Paralleling the wing margins are two rows of blue chevrons below a row of orange spots. It is amazing how such a somber butterfly is actually a beautiful blend of sedate tones.

The Red-spotted Purple's cream-colored caterpillar is humped with a darker saddle, making it look like a bird dropping. The larvae also have two stubby bristles extending from behind the head. They hibernate as larvae but still manage to turn out three broods a year. The pupa is whitish-gray with dark streaks and a silver mark, but the saddle and abdomen are brown.

The adults will visit carrion as readily as flowers or sap. A fresh pile of dung is as appetizing to a Red-spotted as is rotting fruit in an orchard. But don't be surprised to find Red snooping around your garden.

Male Red-spotted Purples are lazy suitors. They prefer to perch on treetops with a good view of the area and potential mates. On the approach of an unidentified object they will dart out to investigate. Once the proper attention has been given to the trespasser, the Red quickly resumes its post.

This collection of red, white, and blue is a fine specimen to encounter on any day. Red-spotted Purples are said to be a subspecies of the White-banded Admiral. When the two are mated, the offspring may show varying amounts of white on the wings. Then again, they may have full bars, simply a few white dots, or perhaps no white at all.

Range: *Canada to the Gulf and from the Atlantic to Arizona.*

ATTRACTED TO:
carrion, dung, flowers,
sap and rotting fruit

Euptoieta claudia

VARIEGATED FRITILLARY

ariegated means having a diversity of colors or having discrete markings of different colors, an appropriate description of this member of the Fritillary family. It is more tawny than the others in its group but still retains the black zigzag pattern. From the upper side, black spots are noticeable along the inside margin of both wings. They do lack the silvery spots generally associated with the larger Fritillaries. The underside is, however, an interesting concoction of whitish-browns, with a good dose of orange on the bottom half of the forewing. It sounds as complicated as it looks, but it helps the Variegated Fritillary hide among vegetation. The two-and-a-half-inch wingspan makes it midsize as Frits go. The males prefer to fly low to the ground in a swift, darting pattern when patrolling for females.

The cream-colored eggs give birth to one of the more attractive caterpillars in the United States. The reddish-orange larva has white stripes and a black head. There are also six rows of dark spines running the course of the backside, with the forward pair being larger.

Differing from the other true Fritillaries, the Variegated Frits use a wider selection of host plants than their relatives. Where the others use only violas, Variegated Fritillaries will consume passionflowers, pansies, stonecrop, and plantain. The chrysalis is a real jewel to encounter in the field. It is a shiny blue-green, almost reminiscent of mother-of-pearl. They look like they were constructed from the inner surface of an abalone shell. It is then garnished with flecks of gold, orange, and black.

The adults range far and wide and are regular visitors to gardens. They will gladly visit many wild or domestic flowers but are just a happy with dung or carrion. Variegateds mainly inhabit the southern tier of the U.S. but will venture near the Canadian border during the summer months.

Range: *Throughout the U.S., except for the Pacific Northwest.*

ATTRACTED TO:
*passionflowers, pansies,
stonecrop, plantain,
dung, carrion and violas*

Limenitis archippus

VICEROY

xperts will argue this all day: Does the Viceroy gain protection by mimicking the poisonous milkweed butterflies, or does it actually taste like week-old roadkill? The debate may go on forever, with no one ever knowing for sure.

On the wing, Viceroys are discernible from Monarchs only by their flight pattern. A few rapid beats, then a glide. A couple more, then glide. The flight of the Monarch is deliberate. The Viceroy will rest with its wings only partially closed, while the Monarch keeps them together. Those who venture close enough will see the thin black line passing through veins on the hindwings. The line parallels the hindwing margin and is very noticeable when the Viceroy is at rest. That is if you could get close enough to view this field mark. For everyone else, they look like a smaller version of the black-veined, orange-winged Monarch.

The tips of willow and aspen leaves serve as delivery rooms for the greenish-yellow oval eggs. The larvae do a wonderful impersonation of bird droppings. They can be greenish or brown, but they always have a white saddle. They also have two thick horns and little bumps scattered around the body. The caterpillars prepare a winter home by rolling a leaf into a tube and securing it with silk. Then the third instar larva hibernates inside until spring. The chrysalides are even passed by because of their resemblance to avian dung. There are three broods in southern areas, but latitude is always a deciding factor for numbers produced.

Viceroys will visit sap and dung as quickly as flowers but are readily found in the garden. They will also sup on the honeydew of aphids and on moist, decaying wood.

Range: *North America from the Great Basin to the Atlantic and from Canada to the Gulf.*

ATTRACTED TO:
*sap, dung, aphids
and decaying wood*

Polygonia zephyrus

Zephyr Comma

he Zephyr wears a silver symbol of its name on its wings. And being one of the Anglewings, it shares several other traits common to the group. The orange wings are flecked with black dots, but just slightly. The purple edging of the Question Mark is absent, replaced with broken dashes. The hindwings still terminate into the tell-tale points that are common to the species. Charcoal-gray below with only a nuance of grayish-white smudging serves it well as camouflage when it is resting on the ground. Closer inspection reveals a faint silver crescent on the backwing.

The eggs of the Zephyr can be found on rhododendrons as often as they can be found on elms or currants. The larvae are black, with reddish spines toward the front and white ones toward the rear. Pink and olive seem like unlikely colors for a chrysalis, but tell that to the Zephyr. It seems happy with its Miami Beach art-deco color theme, and even spices it up a little more with silver studs. The adult emerges in only about fourteen days, but the number of broods is uncertain. Zephyrs overwinter in the adult stages, as do the others of this family. On the first warm day above fifty-five degrees they will be on the wing.

The Zephyr is a quick and agile aerialist. When startled, it will bolt for the safety of wooded edges, but ironically it will soon return to the same spot. They are not shy about visiting flowers and may be enticed by asters, buddleia, and wildflowers. It is the overgrown or wooded garden that the Zephyr finds most attractive. Although it is wonderfully camouflaged, it never ventures far from its sanctuary.

The Zephyr occupies the ecological niche left vacant by the Question Marks, Satyrs, Commas, and Fawns. In the western mountains it is the most common of all of its relatives. From early spring until late autumn, Zephyrs can be found along streams, trails, or visiting meadow flowers. But this hardy polygonia can even make its home above the tree line.

Range: *British Columbia to Mexico and eastward into the Sierras.*

Attracted to:
*rhododendrons, elm,
currant, asters, buddleia
and wildflowers*

Pieris rapae

CABBAGE WHITE

his may be the most famous of all the North American butter-flies, though it is not a native species. It was introduced to Quebec in 1860 but decided not to stay. In less than 100 years it could be found everywhere in the country. Unfortunately, its spectacular success has been the scourge of farmers and gardeners ever since. It is the only butterfly in the United States officially declared a pest by the U.S. Department of Agriculture.

The Cabbage White's pale yellow eggs can be found on cabbage, mustards, and, most often, on nasturtiums. A female is capable of laying up to 700 eggs in her lifetime. Covered with a short, fine pile, the emerging bright-green larva sports yellow back and side stripes. Usually found on the leaf surface of its host, it will eagerly bore deep into the heads of cabbage.

The pupa of the Cabbage White varies from green to mottled brown or gray, depending on its background. There are many broods in the South but only three in the North. It hibernates in the pupal stage, and is usually one of the first butterflies on the wing in spring.

The adults are white with black wing tips and wing spots. These dots are the distinguishing marks between the sexes. The males have one black dot on the forewing, while the females have two. They are located slightly off center of the forewing.

Male Cabbage Whites prefer to seek females near host plants. If the male locates a receptive lady friend, they may be seen traveling about, intertwined in the throes of mating. If the male is not successful, he may fall prey to the spiral dance, the butterfly version of a brush-off. The partners spiral upwards, circling each other. Sometimes the pair reaches great heights before the female folds its wings and drops to the vegetation below. The jilted suitor is left starry-eyed and alone in its ecstasy flight.

Range: *Entire continental United States.*

ATTRACTED TO:
clover, nasturtium, cabbage and mustards

Pontia protodice

CHECKERED WHITE

The Checkered White was probably more numerous during Colonial times than it is now, because modern agricultural methods forced this native to vacate its former haunts. Some blame it on the encroachment of the Cabbage White, while others disagree.

The Checkered White's fast, skipping flight is distinctive. Although its adult life may be as short as a week, it disperses quickly, forming colonies many miles away. It can readily be found at roadsides as well as in gardens and meadows.

The spindle-shaped eggs of the Checkered White are laid on the leaves of mustards and cabbages both wild and cultivated. The yellow egg turns orange just before the larva makes an appearance. The bluish-green caterpillar is sprinkled with black among its yellow longitudinal stripes. The overwintering chrysalis is also blue-green, with flecks of black. There are several broods in most places, but they seem to be year-round in parts of California.

Overall, the color patterns of the Checkered White can vary endlessly, and the checkering is far more prominent on the female. From there things become confusing. Spring broods are marked heavier than later broods. Summer males may be all white, with the checkering almost unnoticeable. Or at any time they may have a gray, olive, or tan tint to the wing scales. To complicate matters even more, Western Whites vary from Eastern Whites. And those variations don't include interbreeding and hybrids' contribution to an ever-increasing pattern frenzy.

This does not seem to present a problem to the abundant Whites, which locate a proper mate through the use of ultraviolet light. Males lack the pheromone-producing scales common to other Whites. Hence, the male wing pattern absorbs ultraviolet and the female's reflects it. Some "bloom years" can produce huge numbers of Checkered Whites. The Checkered White can be found in various habitats from gardens to vacant fields and everywhere in between.

Range: *Most of United States except for the Pacific Northwest.*

ATTRACTED TO:
mustards, cabbages and clover

Colias philodice

COMMON (OR CLOUDED) SULPHUR

I have trouble calling any butterfly common. So we will use the other name of this little beauty, the Clouded Sulphur. It ranges throughout the U.S. but is more familiar in the East.

The males are bright yellow above, with sharp black borders. The females have a mottled border that is not as clearly defined. Some females may even be white smudged with black. But as a rule, the females usually have less black on the wing margins than the males.

The chartreuse eggs are deposited on any of a number of legumes, especially clover. The bright green caterpillars have a lighter-colored side stripe, and a darker stripe on their back. Because of its diverse diet, the Clouded Sulphur has become widespread and it produces several broods per year. In the northern reaches the green chrysalis is used for overwintering.

The Clouded Sulphur interbreeds with its cousin, the Orange Sulphur, which may produce unusual color patterns. Some offspring may have orange on only half of the wing. Others may be albino, with pink wing fringes. The possible color combinations are endless.

Clouded Sulphur males are extremely fond of puddle clubbing. In many areas it is not unusual to find them congregating on and around the eyes of turtles and alligators to drink the tears of their host. Actually, only the males do this. The saline solution assists the males in the production of sperm. Originally a northeastern species, Clouded Sulphurs are now found everywhere in the nation except for Florida.

Clouded Sulphurs are very attracted to the garden, where they collect nectar from a variety of flowers. Dandelion, phlox, clover, and milkweeds are all favored by the Clouded Sulphur.

Every Sulphur is like a square inch of sunlight with a pleasant attitude.

Range: *Any open space throughout the United States, with the exception of Florida.*

ATTRACTED TO:
dandelion, phlox, clover, milkweed and legumes

Phoebis sennae

CLOUDLESS SULPHUR

The Giant or Cloudless Sulphur is aptly named for its impressive size. The large yellow wings are quite the show-stopper. Wherever wild senna is found, there will be a sight like no other. The enormous golden wings of the Cloudless Sulphur play like leaves in the gentle autumn wind. Bouncing and bobbing, they appear to change their minds in mid-flap and switch directions.

Male Cloudless Sulphurs are lemon yellow, while the female can range from golden to white. The females have a dark-colored dot that is slightly off center on the upper surface of the forewing. During their seasonal migration, some individuals fly as far north as New York, while others make it all the way west to the Rockies. Except for the extremists, the migrations are usually round-trip.

The white eggs of the Cloudless Sulphur turn pale orange prior to the caterpillar emerging. The larva is green with yellow side stripes, and rows of black dots cross the back. Sometimes it will turn orange before it pupates. They can be found on sennas and on clover.

In many areas along the Gulf Coast of Florida the medians of city streets are planted with cassia. Anyone driving down these avenues is delighted by groups of Giant Sulphurs flitting from tree to tree. With large, sunny yellow wings, they are just a pleasure to watch. There are many broods in the South, but only two in the northern reaches. The chrysalides are quite spectacular, with their angulated triangles of pink or green. They can start as one color but may develop into another as they mature.

Cloudless Sulphurs are attracted to firebush, cardinal flower, lantana, and morning glory for nectar sources, making them eager visitors to gardens. Trying to approach one however, will leave you with only a faraway glimpse of a Giant Sulphur hightailing it to someone else's yard.

Range: *Mexico to southern California and throughout the Midwest to Canada and the Northeast.*

ATTRACTED TO:
*wild senna, cassia,
clover, firebush,
cardinal flower, lantana
and morning glory*

Colias eurydice (California)
Colias cesonia (Southern)

DOGFACE

The Dogface gets its moniker from the wing patterns it proudly wears. On each forewing is the profile of dog's face complete with a black eye. Some people say it resembles a poodle; others say a spaniel. The California Dogface is also called the Flying Pansy because of the yellow, black, and pink wings. With wings unfolded, the Dogface is a dead ringer for the garden-variety Pansy. There is even a Mexican Wolf-faced version, which occasionally strays into the U.S. The Southern Dogface does not have the pink of its western cousin but is every bit as beautiful.

The rapid flight of the Dogface is very noticeable as they dart from clover to clover. The underwings are yellow with a small black circle on the forewing and a pink circle on the hindwing.

The pale green egg yields a dull green caterpillar. There is much variation in striping on the larvae, or they may even be plain. However, the larvae are normally striped lengthwise with black and yellow. False indigo or clover is where to find them.

The chrysalis is also green, but with a lateral white line at the abdomen. In some areas they may overwinter as adults; in other areas they hibernate as pupae. The winter form emerges with an overall magenta blush. The burgundy tinge is a result of cold temperatures during the pupal stage. The Dogface produces several annual broods that all have particular variations.

The Dogface is very attracted to clovers, thistle, and composites and they are at home in a variety of habitats. Preferring a warmer climate, the Dogface can be found as far south as Argentina. Wherever you find one of these precious jewels, they will always bring a smile to your face.

California not only made the Dogface the state butterfly, it was also honored on a U.S. postage stamp in 1976.

Range: *California to Florida and up through the Midwest to Canada.*

ATTRACTED TO:
false indigo, clover, thistle and composites

Eurema lisa

LITTLE SULPHUR

he Little Sulphur or Little Yellow is fairly common east of the Rockies. In Latin it is called *E. lisa*, a pretty name for a pretty butterfly. Despite having a wingspan of an inch and a half, this flaxen fairy is capable of long flights. It ranges from Canada to Central America, but the Little Yellow cannot tolerate northern winters. Its population must be replenished every year by flights from the southern extent of its range.

Little Sulphurs migrate in vast numbers throughout the Caribbean and southern Atlantic regions. Columbus reported large numbers of these tiny beauties passing by the deck of the Santa Maria on his voyage to the New World.

The light-green egg produces a caterpillar that never gets more than three-quarters of an inch long. Covered with a fine pile, the green larvae have white side stripes and a dark dorsal stripe. It eventually becomes the typical triangular style chrysalis of Sulphurs. The green pupa look like someone sprinkled it with black pepper. As with the other Sulphurs, the chrysalis is always positioned on a stem by the mid-dorsal girdle.

This tiny golden glider is lemon-yellow with sharp black wing margins. When at rest the wings are held together, exposing an orange spot on the apex of the hindwing at the point where it intersects with the forewing. The remainder of the underside is yellow-green, but it looks like it's been smudged with darker colors. Although legumes and clover are their primary hosts, Little Sulphurs will readily take nectar from garden flowers.

The males patrol all day searching for females. They investigate any possibilities, but they avoid any other butterflies with wing bars. Not totally unsociable, they will visit puddle clubs to catch up on butterfly business.

Range: *East of the Rockies. Canada to Costa Rica and into the Caribbean.*

ATTRACTED TO:
*legumes, clover
and garden flowers*

Colias eurytheme

ORANGE SULPHUR

The Orange Sulphur is also known as the Alfalfa Butterfly. Although there are great color and pattern variations within the species, there is always some amount of orange present. Many times this is the only way to distinguish between them and the Clouded Sulphurs. It adapts well to changing agricultural practices and continues to increase its range. The Alfalfa has a taste for garden as well as farm plants. In meadows they mingle with the other Sulphurs and Whites.

The long white eggs can be found on clover, alfalfa, vetch, and lupine. The eggs turn scarlet prior to hatching. As with all Sulphurs, the females are always in a hurry. Eggs can be found on either the bottoms or tops of leaves. No time to pay any mind to particulars, she lays an egg and she's on her way.

Orange Sulphur caterpillars are grass-green, with a dark stripe down the back and a whitish one down each side. Pink stripes may appear low on the sides. The larvae eventually form a green chrysalis that may have flecks of yellow or black. There are as many as four broods a year.

The range of the Alfalfa is ever-increasing. It may be one of the few butterflies with a population that is actually increasing. Adaptability to changing farming methods, interbreeding, and a strong flight has assured this little jewel success in today's world. As with the Clouded Sulphur, Orange Sulphurs are only held in check by the oceans and the Great White North.

The females do not have a preference for either orange or yellow males. The choice of mates is governed by the amount of ultraviolet light reflected by the male's wing. This ability is restricted to the males, who are repelled at the sight of ultraviolet wings. Pheromones also assist in the female's final decision in choosing the correct mate.

Range: *From Canada to Mexico and from the Atlantic to the Pacific.*

ATTRACTED TO:
*clover, alfalfa,
vetch and lupine*

Strymon melinus

GRAY HAIRSTREAK

he Gray is probably the most common of all the Hairstreaks in the country. It is also called the Cotton Borer, and at times the larvae can be so numerous they are considered pests.

The name Hairstreak comes from the thin lines on the underside of the wings. Gray Hairstreaks are smaller butterflies, with a wingspan of less than an inch and a half. Fine filaments protrude from the hindwings, which act as a defense mechanism. When at rest, the hair-like strands project. As a predator approaches, the tails are mistaken for antennae and they break off easily, allowing the Hairstreak a chance to escape. The filaments will not grow back, but at least the Gray Hairstreak has two chances for survival.

The Gray has a fancy for cotton, mallows, and a sweet tooth for strawberries, all plants they seek as nurseries for their pale green eggs. Their larval colors range from pink to reddish browns, usually with mauve, green, or white side stripes. Opportunists, the larvae have been reported to use up to fifty different species of plants as host. The pupa is a mixture of brown and black. The Gray Hairstreak hibernates as a chrysalis to emerge early in the spring.

Above, the males are a deep shade of slate gray, while the female are more brown. There is a prominent orange spot, and an inconspicuous blue dot on the margin of the hindwings. The grayish color is darker in earlier broods than in later ones. But at any time of the year, the males are darker than the females.

The males are late risers and prefer to pursue females during the afternoon. They are extremely swift flyers and happily drop in on gardens for nectar. Except for the extreme north, the Gray Hairstreak is well distributed throughout the country. With two broods north, and more in the south, they can be readily found in vacant lots, fields, or in the woods. They have been doing especially well in southeastern California, where they interbreed with other Hairstreaks.

Range: *The entire U.S.*

ATTRACTED TO:
cotton, mallow and strawberries

Phyciodes tharos

PEARL CRESCENTSPOT

It may be small, but the Pearl Crescentspot is a mighty-mite that seems to be everywhere. The Pearl is probably one of the most common butterflies in the country. Its habits and smaller size help to keep it fairly inconspicuous. The flight pattern is very low because it prefers to stay among the vegetation. Darting from stem to stem keeps it protected from hungry eyes.

Invade its territory and you will be attacked. The males prefer standing sentry on blades of grass or branches for females rather than patrolling. When anything enters the forbidden zone, Pearly just has to dart out to investigate. Humans are not given any quarter and come under close scrutiny, after which the pugnacious little sentinel returns to his post.

The eggs of the Pearl Crescentspot are laid in clusters on the leaves of asters. The brown or black caterpillar is covered with yellow dots and yellow bands along the sides. It also has many branching spines which may be yellow to yellowish-brown. The larvae feed lazily and socially, never constructing a web. Eventually they become chrysalides of either yellow, brown, or gray, and many have stripes and patches of various colors.

Less than two inches across, the orange wings are a patchwork of black markings. The forewings have black tips and a scrambling of black patches and zigzags. The hindwings are not as busy, but have a row of black dots paralleling the black border. The female's wings are marked more delicately above than the male. Underneath, the forewing is pale orange with some black patterning. The hindwing is a potpourri of cream and yellow patches. Along the border is maroon surrounding the famous crescent-moon-shaped mark.

This most common butterfly is an ardent visitor to gardens and will quickly nectar from flowers. If you have asters you will probably have Pearlies.

Range: *Canada to Mexico and from the Statue of Liberty to the Golden Gate Bridge.*

ATTRACTED TO:
asters

Everes comyntas (*Eastern*)
Everes amyntula (*Western*)

TAILED BLUE

he Tailed Blues come in two varieties: Eastern and Western. The major difference between the two is the more distinctive marking on the underside of the Eastern. The Western enjoys locoweed and vetch, whereas the Eastern larvae eat clovers and beans. They are small butterflies with wingspans of just over an inch. The adults are blue above, with the female usually being a little darker. The white fringe outlining the wings are complemented with a thin black border. Underneath, these little lapis gems are silvery-gray with black dots and dashes. Most curiously, a thread-like projection protrudes from the hindwings and deceives would-be predators. An orange dot with a black center at the base of the wing completes the charade, directing a predator's aim to this area instead of to a vital point, allowing escape.

The eggs of the Tailed Blue are often laid inside flower buds or on the stems. The larvae of both Easterns and Westerns are similar but may vary by shades of green. The Eastern has brown stripes down the side and the Western has purple. The larvae of some species of Blue secrete a fluid known as honeydew, an elixir highly prized by ants, who will readily attend the larvae in exchange for this treat. It is the equivalent of an entomological protection racket. One of those you-scratch-my-exoskeleton-and-I'll-scratch-yours arrangements. The overwintering caterpillar slumbers away inside the host plants. The chrysalides are hairy and can be tan to creamy. The Eastern Tailed Blue enjoys three broods, but its Western relative only has two.

One of the most abundant butterflies, the Tailed Blue can be found in gardens or along roadsides. The delicate tails of the Blue twitch dramatically as they nectar, directing all attention their way. This may be the only field mark a novice may have to distinguish the Tailed from the Spring Azure. They are both as fond of puddles as they are of gardens.

Range: *Throughout the country. The two populations meet at the Rocky Mountains.*

ATTRACTED TO:
*locoweed, vetch, clover
and beans*

Celastrina ladon

Spring Azure

Common throughout the entire United States, this little cerulean chip is always there to welcome the spring. The violet-blue adults take to the wing earlier than most of their cousins to assure us that warmer days have finally returned. Adults born earlier in the year tend to be darker hued than their children. Those born later are naturally lighter. All males have blackened forewing tips that dissolve into a checkered pattern on the hind margin. The wing borders on the females are thin black lines just inside the fringed white edge. Underneath, the wings are shades of gray separated by faint black markings.

The eggs of the Spring Azure are laid inside flowers, providing the new larvae with their favorite delicacy. The larvae can vary considerably in color from cream to rose, with some becoming shades of green. These variations are governed by seasonal and geographic influences.

Usually the caterpillar has a mid-dorsal line of green or brown. The larvae secretes "honeydew" through an opening on the back. Ants will tend and protect these little meal tickets in exchange for this protein-rich food. Normally an item on the ant's menu, Spring Azures can buy their freedom with a few drops of dew. Caterpillars prefer to eat the flowers of dogwood, blueberry, and viburnum.

The color of the chrysalides varies, and changes with the time of the year. Earlier pupae are pale and later ones are darker. Ranging from tan to brown, the chrysalides may be found on a stem or in leaf litter. There are multiple broods every year, with the last one of the season overwintering.

The Spring Azure has itchy wings and could never wait for spring. So at the first sign of warmer days, it breaks out of its thin prison for the freedom of the sky. The Spring Azure is most at home along roadsides, in fields, and near open woods. Males police for females near shrubs but will take to mud and dung at break time.

Range: *Throughout North America.*

ATTRACTED TO:
*nasturtium, dogwood,
blueberry and viburnum*

Epargyreus clarus

SILVER-SPOTTED SKIPPER

It may not be one of the most beautiful butterflies in the country, but it deserves attention. The Skippers are distinguished from the other butterflies by the shape of their antennae. Butterflies have antennae that are thin, straight, and end in a bulb. The antennae of the Skippers become slightly thicker toward the ends and curve into a hook.

The Silver-spotted, just like other Skippers, seems to be the missing link between butterflies and moths. They are generally drab, the body is stocky, and the flight is erratic and swift. Their flight is similar to a stone skipping across a pond. Hence the name, Skippers.

The Silver-spotted has one of the most extensive ranges of all the butterflies and is equally at home in the woods or garden. The two-inch, dark brown forewings are marked with yellowish-orange spots in the center. The hindwing is an unmarked uniform brown. From the underside, the golden spots show through the forewing, offsetting the distinctive silver patch of the hindwing.

Green and globular, the eggs of the Silver-spotted Skipper will be found on locusts, wisteria, and legumes. The yellowish-green caterpillar has two orange eyespots on an enlarged brown head. For a home, the larvae cuts circular areas from the leaf edges of the host plant, folds them back, and holds them in place with silk. As the caterpillar grows, it adds a second leaf. Unlike the other butterflies, this dark brown pupa is encased in a loose cocoon among the leaf litter. The winter is passed in this stage of development.

There is only one brood in the North, and possibly three in the South. The males seem to prefer searching for females in the morning. Any habitat is okay by the Silver-spotted and it can be found in most. Roadsides, meadows, and gardens are all familiar haunts of this Skipper.

Range: *Few places in the U.S. are without the Silver-spotted Skipper.*

ATTRACTED TO:
*locusts, wisteria,
legumes and mallow*

Pyrgus communis

CHECKERED SKIPPER

The Checkered Skipper is the most common and the most beautiful of all Lepidoptera known as Skippers. The upper surface may be charcoal-gray to black, with white checkering seeming to form into dark bands. The fringe outlining both wings is checkered in gray, white, and black. the body is covered with wonderful hair-like scales that reflect a bluish halo in the sunlight. The underside pattern is as variable as it is above. Generally the designs are alternating wavy rows of tan, green, or white. The patterns of the females are bolder than those of the males.

The greenish egg of the Checkered Skipper changes to a creamy color right before hatching. Mallows are the host plant of choice for this little checkered wonder. The caterpillars are shades of brown, from tan to coffee. There is a dark stripe down the back, and brown and white side stripes starting at the black head and running aft. There is also a coat of thick white hairs along the course of the body. Coloration of the chrysalis can be as variable as it is in the other stages. More often than not, they are green at the head, which resolves to brown toward the tip. The broods are continuous in the South, but in the northern areas they may diapause and overwinter as pupa. Below the Mason-Dixon Line, they may spend winters hibernating as full-grown larva.

Checkered Skippers can be found from field to roadside as well as in the garden. Adults are very fond of nectaring from hollyhock, mimosa, New England aster, and zinnias. Unlike many of their cousins, the Checkered Skipper likes to sun with its wings out flat at its sides, as opposed to the conventional above-the-body style most butterflies have adopted.

The flight of Checkered Skippers is short, fast, and direct. The males are noted for their pugnacity when patrolling a very strict beat.

Range: *Common throughout the United States, Canada, and Mexico.*

ATTRACTED TO:
*hollyhock, mimosa,
New England aster,
zinnias and mallows*

Agraulis vanillae

GULF FRITILLARY

s it a tropical butterfly or is it a common one? is the first question asked about this little beauty. The only thing that the Gulf Fritillary seems to have in common with other Fritillaries is perhaps the silver on the underside of the wings. It seems to fit more in the Heliconia family, whose members have wings that are twice as long as they are wide.

As with others in this group, the Gulf Fritillary is toxic to some predators because of its larval diet. They generally go undisturbed because their color pattern is recognized by predators as a sign of danger. One of three truly exotic looking butterflies in the U.S., the Gulf Fritillary looks like it would be more at home in a rain forest. To see this magnificent insect on the wing is simply spectacular. The three-inch wings flash orange on the down-stroke and silver and red on the upsweep.

The long, narrow wings are brilliant orange above, with just a touch of black dots on the forewing. At the midpoint of the leading edge are three black dots with white centers. On the hindwing, the dots become black circles along the border. Underneath, the Gulf Fritillary is a thing of real beauty. The forewing is brown-tipped, with large silver dots. The remainder is bright reddish-orange, with silver dots encircled by black. The hindwing is brown, with large silver spots.

The Gulf Fritillary's yellow egg is oblong, ribbed, and deposited only on members of the Passiflora family. The spiny brown caterpillars are lined with red and cream-colored dots. The long, curved chrysalis can be brown or greenish-brown, with assorted patches of gray or brown. There are two small horns on the head and the rest is covered in warts, which completes the disguise. In the South there are three broods. Neither the host plant nor the butterfly can tolerate northern winters.

Range: *Generally from the lower half of the country coast to coast. During the summer, the Gulf Fritillary migrates northward, reaching the Upper Midwest as far as and into Minnesota.*

ATTRACTED TO:
passiflora and violet

Heliconius charitonius

ZEBRA LONGWING

o butterfly in the United States can be confused with the Zebra Longwing. The elongated ebony wings are brilliantly striped with yellow. The underside is similar, except for crimson spots near the base of both wings. The flight pattern is slow and weak. Watching the Zebra for a while brings up the question of how it could even stay aloft. The feeble flaps, however, become a darting escape at the approach of predators.

The ribbed yellow eggs will only be found on toxic passiflora, which render the larvae undesirable to predators. The caterpillars are real works of art; the pure white larva is transversed with rows of black dots. And there are six rows of black spines on this nocturnal feeder. The chrysalis looks like it could be Hades' gate-keeper. Long and thin, the pupa has two antler-like projections on the head, which is a gruesome rendition of a devil's face. Twisted and distorted, the mottled brown sleeping chamber would easily be passed over by a predator. Many broods are produced in the warmer climates, but the Zebra can not tolerate less than subtropical temperatures.

Not only unusual in its appearance, the Zebra Longwing also displays many eccentricities. Unlike its North American relatives, adult Zebras can use pollen as a source of food. The pollen is first collected on the proboscis. Then a small amount of fluid is released to dissolve it into a drinkable liquid. The solution is rich with protein that affords the individual the ability to live long and prosper. Adults live for several months, allowing the female to lay up to 1,000 eggs.

The males are attracted to the pupae of females by a scent. The impatient suitor does not even wait for her to emerge. He opens her chrysalis just enough to mate. A drop of pheromone repellent is then left at the scene to discourage others. Considered one of the most intelligent butterflies, they prefer to roost communally at night.

Range: *The lower half of the United States from the Carolinas to California.*

ATTRACTED TO:
passiflora and pollen

GARDEN BUTTERFLIESS OF NORTH AMERICA

BUTTERFLIES ON THE WORLD WIDE WEB

Visit Rick Mikula on the web! With more than 4,000 visitors daily, the Butterfly Web Site is the oldest and largest site devoted to butterflies. It has over 1,500 pages of information regarding every aspect of lepidopteran life. Conservation, gardening, natural history and farming are only a few of the many topics covered. The Butterfly Web Site has won numerous awards for its quality and educational value. It has helped many institutions world-wide with the advancement of the public's understanding of lepidoptera. The information is free to the public and can be downloaded by teachers, students and families to aid in their appreciation of butterflies. Catch some butterflies on the Net today!

http://www.isit.com/butterfly/